TEACHERS' TREASURY

by Imogene Forte

Incentive Publications, Inc.
Nashville, Tennessee

Cover by Susan Eaddy
Illustrations by Gayle Seaberg Harvey

ISBN 0-86530-067-4

Table of Contents

ENRICHMENT

TERRIFIC TEACHING TIPS

TOOLBOX

ABOUT THIS BOOK

Teachers of primary children are very special people. TEACHERS' TREASURY is designed to help make classroom time "prime time" and to make the teacher's classroom time easier and more exciting. Included are:

- classroom perk-ups
- communicators and awards
- construction projects
- cooperative learning projects
- experiments and explorations
- individual and group activities and projects

- puzzles and games
- reading and writing exercises
- ready-to-use worksheets
- research and library activities
- skills-based and enrichment lessons
- study guides

Divided into language arts, math, science, social studies and enrichment sections, the lessons and projects you need to liven up a humdrum day are here. Each section is prefaced by a unique silhouette design for use as a booklet cover, poster, bulletin board, or learning center display. All the activities are easy to plan for and implement and require little or no special classroom materials.

A special bonus teachers' toolbox section filled with terrific teaching tips includes: theme days, health fair, friendship jigsaw puzzles, globe-making, clothesline art exhibit, drama, art projects, happy homework suggestions and more.

This treasury has been compiled to add fun and excitement to your lesson planning and provide you and your students with many golden, memory-making learning experiences.

LANGUAGE ARTS

NAME GAME
Word Usage Game
LANGUAGE ARTS

Print words that the students are using in content area reading (social studies, science, etc.) on index cards and print their definitions on other index cards. Place the words in one box and the definitions in another. Make an answer key by writing the words and their definitions on a piece of paper. Place the answer key in an envelope to be taped to one of the boxes. Instruct the students to match the words and definitions and to check themselves against the answer key.

MATCH-UPS
Vocabulary Activity
LANGUAGE ARTS

No word in any language is more important to an individual than his or her name. Next time you need a language "pepper-upper," try this name game. Instruct the students as follows:

1) Write your name across the top of a piece of paper.
2) Write parts of speech down the side of the paper. (Provide an example such as the one below.)
3) Cut words out of newspapers, junk mail and magazines that begin with the letters of your name and that may be classified as the designated parts of speech.
4) Glue the words in the appropriate spaces.

Part of Speech	S	A	L	L	Y
Noun					
Verb					
Adjective					

Fun With Anagrams

In this game, students are to rearrange given letters to spell two or more words. Write the letters (see the suggestions below) on a chart or chalkboard for a teacher-directed game, on index cards for individual free-time use, or on a worksheet to be reproduced and distributed to each student. After several experiences with this game, students may enjoy working in pairs or teams to discover more words.

Suggested letters to use for starters:

proe:	rope, pore	cfae:	face, cafe
levid:	devil, lived	refe:	free, reef
otol:	loot, tool	nrage:	range, anger
deir:	ride, dire	ateh:	heat, hate
aret:	rate, tear,	lsat:	salt, slat, last
ipns:	spin, nips, snip, pins	amet:	mate, tame, team, meat
olop:	loop, pool	aceth:	teach, cheat
aefr:	fear, fare	loct:	colt, clot
tsho:	shot, host	aerc:	care, race

Antonyms Anyone?

Write antonyms on the chalkboard in two columns. Ask each student to select a pair of antonyms and to use the antonyms in a sentence to show their contrasting meanings.

Example: A tiny mouse was riding on a huge elephant's back.

Give each student one point for each sentence in which the antonyms are used correctly. The student with the most points after a given time period wins the game.

Suggested antonyms:

alike	distant	different	near
beautiful	fat	ugly	thin
blunt	foolish	sharp	wise
buy	heavy	sell	light
calm	loose	excited	tight
danger	powerful	safety	weak

SOUND-ALIKE BOX
Beginning Sounds Activity/Game
LANGUAGE ARTS

Cover a shoe box with self-adhesive paper, gift wrap or wallpaper. Label the box "Sound-Alikes" and place articles such as the following in it: pencil, spoon, fork, knife (plastic utensils are fine), eraser, small book, etc. Instruct the students to select objects from the box one at a time and to name another object for each which has the same beginning sound. Use the box as an independent free-time activity, a game for pairs of students to play verbally, or a learning center activity (have the students write the object names and "sound-alike" words on paper).

APPLES FOR THE TEACHER
Beginning Sounds Activity/Game
LANGUAGE ARTS

Place a tree branch in a flowerpot and anchor it with small rocks. Cut apples out of red construction paper and print vocabulary words or familiar words on the apples. Punch a hole in each apple and run yarn through the holes to make loops for hanging the apples on the tree. Let each student remove an apple from the tree after naming another word with the same beginning sound as the word written on the apple. Pairs or small groups of students can complete the activity as a free-time learning game. The students with the most apples is the winner. To adapt the activity for a learning center, provide instructions and extra paper on which the students may write the words.

Never throw away the comics section of the newspaper — especially four-color comics! Start a collection of comics and ask students to bring extra copies from home so that you will have an abundance of comics for class activities such as those below.

1.   Cut apart the individual "panels" of a comic strip and place them in an envelope. Instruct the students to arrange the panels in the proper sequence to tell the "story."

2.   Cut out the captions from several comic strips and have the students write or recite creative dialogue.

3.   Omit the final panel of each of several comic strips and instruct the students to develop original "endings."

4.   Give each student an "uncut" comic strip and ask him or her to develop a "follow-up" comic based on the characters and the situation.

5.   Have the students work in groups to "act out" comic strips before the rest of the class. Ask the class members of the "audience" to describe something that could happen next.

Puzzles, mazes and games serve to break the monotony of the school day and challenge students to use thinking skills in the truest sense. They can be lifesavers for those ten to fifteen minute breaks in the schedule (just before lunch or the last bell, or when all of the planned work is finished early). Sometimes a simple chalkboard project or a verbally-directed game may be just the thing, while at other times high-interest worksheets will serve better. The reproducible worksheets on the following pages will serve as starters as you build up a collection of your own.

Suggested word search puzzle topics might include:

weather words		jungle animals	means of transportation	
hot	frost	tiger	bus	yacht
cold	balmy	lion	car	jeep
humid	ice	elephant	airplane	snowmobile
dry	icicles	ape	train	spaceship
rainy	chilly	chimpanzee	boat	wagon
sunny	cool	hippopotamus	motorcycle	van
snowy	hail	giraffe	bicycle	
freezing	sleet	jaguar		
temperature	flood	snake		
fog	meteorologist	panther		

Suggested crossword puzzle topics might include:

careers and their definitions
sports figures and their respective sports
famous people and what they are famous for
inventors and inventions
states and capitols
analogies
synonyms, homonyms

EXACT WORD FIND
LANGUAGE ARTS

Name _____

Find and circle 22 words beginning with the
   letters ex.
Use the longest and the shortest circled words
   to finish the sentences below.
If you do not know the meaning of a word, look
   up the word in a dictionary.

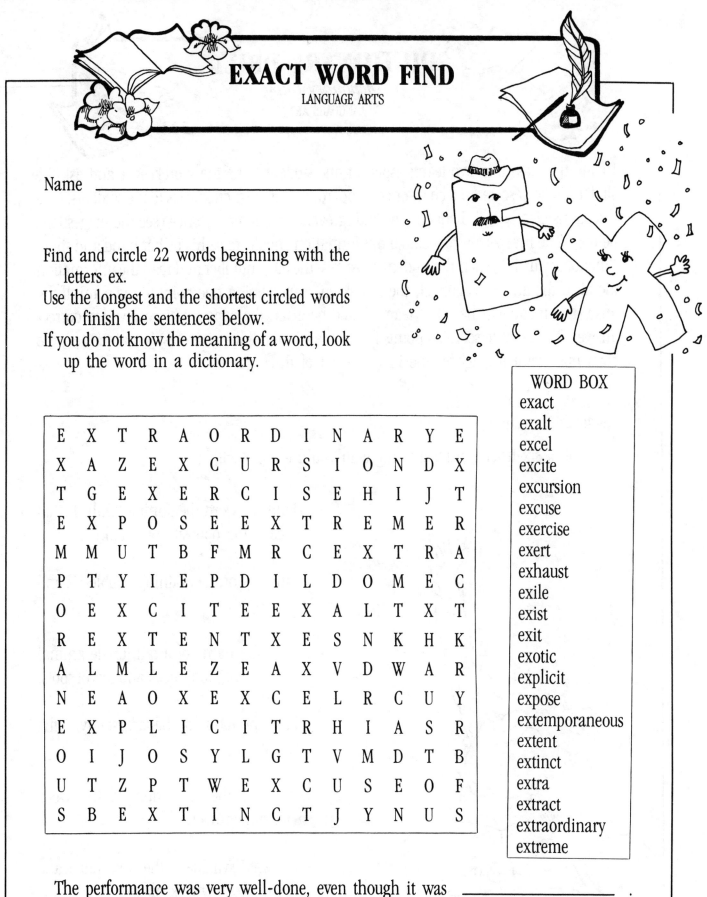

E	X	T	R	A	O	R	D	I	N	A	R	Y	E
X	A	Z	E	X	C	U	R	S	I	O	N	D	X
T	G	E	X	E	R	C	I	S	E	H	I	J	T
E	X	P	O	S	E	E	X	T	R	E	M	E	R
M	M	U	T	B	F	M	R	C	E	X	T	R	A
P	T	Y	I	E	P	D	I	L	D	O	M	E	C
O	E	X	C	I	T	E	E	X	A	L	T	X	T
R	E	X	T	E	N	T	X	E	S	N	K	H	K
A	L	M	L	E	Z	E	A	X	V	D	W	A	R
N	E	A	O	X	E	X	C	E	L	R	C	U	Y
E	X	P	L	I	C	I	T	R	H	I	A	S	R
O	I	J	O	S	Y	L	G	T	V	M	D	T	B
U	T	Z	P	T	W	E	X	C	U	S	E	O	F
S	B	E	X	T	I	N	C	T	J	Y	N	U	S

WORD BOX
exact
exalt
excel
excite
excursion
excuse
exercise
exert
exhaust
exile
exist
exit
exotic
explicit
expose
extemporaneous
extent
extinct
extra
extract
extraordinary
extreme

The performance was very well-done, even though it was _____ .

The theater had only one _____ .

Answer Key

DICTIONARY DRILL
Dictionary Game
LANGUAGE ARTS

Divide the class into two teams. Appoint one student to be the scorekeeper and ask the student to keep score on a chart or chalkboard. Distribute dictionaries to the students. Give directions clearly and distinctly, repeating each direction only once (see the suggestions below). The first person to locate the information should raise his or her hand and shout "dictionary drill." Then the student must give the page number and read the information aloud. If the answer is correct, the scorekeeper may assign one point to the team. If the answer is incorrect, the other team should be given the opportunity to give the correct answer. The team to score 20 points first is the winner. If lively interest is maintained, the class may want to play for the first two out of three games.

Suggested Direction:

- Find a six-letter word beginning with s and ending with t.

- Find a word beginning with l that means the opposite of small.

- Find a word containing double l's and double o's.

- Find the name of a tall jungle animal with a long, long neck and lots of spots.

- Find the name of the largest city in the world.

- What is the definition of the word "extemporaneous"?

- On what syllable of the word hurricane is the accent mark placed?

- Find a synonym for the word *sly*.

HUNTING FOR HEADLINES
Reading Comprehension Activity
LANGUAGE ARTS

Clip news articles out of a local newspaper. (Cut out the appropriate number of articles to meet the students' ability levels.) Cut the headlines off of the articles and put both the articles and headlines in a large envelope. Instruct the students to remove the articles and headlines from the envelope, to read the articles, and to select the correct headline for each article. More mature students may be asked to find the who, what, when and where of the articles and/or to write a different headline for each article.

DIAMOND-SHAPED POETRY
Poetry Writing Activity
LANGUAGE ARTS

Provide the students with brightly-colored construction paper and felt-tip markers or crayons. Write the following poem model on a chart or chalkboard for all to see. Ask each student to write an original diamond-shaped poem on a construction paper diamond. This form of poetry writing is especially interesting when associated with a specific topic of study such as nature, animals, seasons or holidays, a specific country or culture, etc.

Noun 1	Snow
2 words describing noun 1	white, bright
3 words ending in ed or ing	falling, sparkling, shimmering
4 words describing nouns 1 & 2	cold, wet, melting, chilling
3 words ending in ed or ing	driving, blinding, covering
2 words describing noun 2	beautiful, frightening
Noun 2	Blizzard

CIRCUMSTANCES TO WRITE ABOUT
Creative Writing And/Or Discussion Topics
LANGUAGE ARTS

Use these "circumstances" to motivate creative writing or group discussion.

Imagine that . . .

1. You are running away from someone very fast and you are frightened. Who or what are you running from, how do you feel, and what will happen next?

2. You have just been asked to be a passenger on a space flight leaving at midnight tonight. Tell how you feel, what you will decide to do, and what the results of your decision will be.

3. You and your family are on safari in Africa. Write a letter to a classmate telling about the weather, the countryside, the food, the transportation, your daily schedule, and highlights of the experience.

4. You are a scientist who has just made a valuable medical discovery that will save thousands of lives. You are being interviewed for a worldwide radio broadcast. Write about yourself and your work and what you would like to tell the world about it.

5. You have inherited a million dollars that you would like to use to feed hungry children and to provide education for deserving students who otherwise would not be able to attend school. Tell how you will carry out this plan.

GREAT STORY STARTERS

Writing Activity

LANGUAGE ARTS

Write these story starters on a chart, chalkboard or reproducible worksheet to spark students' ideas for creative stories.

1. No one would have dreamed that the dog . . .
2. Stop!
3. If I had a million dollars to spend . . .
4. The angry giant roared . . .
5. Not even the captain could have guessed . . .
6. The boy disappeared in the forest . . .

7. I closed my eyes for just a minute before . . .
8. The girl was no taller than my thumb . . .
9. First one wing and then the other began to fall . . .
10. The school bus came to a sudden stop . . .
11. I sharpened my pencil, opened my notebook and . .
12. Even his best friend wouldn't tell him . . .

13. We hid under the bed . . .
14. I never expected to see a leprechaun, but . . .
15. Every day, the snow piled up deeper and deeper . . .
16. I had the craziest dream . . .
17. Even my best friend wouldn't believe . . .
18. Just as the traffic light turned green . . .

19. The biggest truck I had ever seen appeared suddenly . . .
20. Closer and closer the strange light came toward us . . .
21. A mighty roar of thunder and a flash of lightning . . .
22. The phone rang again and again . . .
23. The strangest sight I've ever seen . . .
24. The rooftops were covered with snow and ice . . .

25. The baby screamed louder and louder . . .
26. Last Halloween . . .
27. Betsy didn't believe in fairy godmothers until . . .
28. Andrew will always remember the day his little brother ran away . . .
29. A giant bee as large as a pony flew out of the forest . . .
30. I have never been so embarrassed . . .

FINISHING UNFINISHED STORIES
Creative Conclusions Writing Activity
LANGUAGE ARTS

Strengthen reading and writing skills by asking the students to write their own titles and endings for unfinished stories. The stories may be presented on a chart or chalkboard or as reproducible worksheets. The important thing to remember when developing the stories is to provide strong context clues and clear characterization while also leaving room for creative interpretation and open-ended plot development.

Examples:

Janet could hardly wait to unwrap the present in the tiny box. Every year she wanted to open the package from Aunt Suzie first. Aunt Suzie seemed to know exactly what Janet wanted. As she blew out the candles on her cake, Janet wondered how Aunt Suzie could keep up with her age when they lived so far apart...

Andy was sadder than he had been in his whole life. He had called and called for Diggy, and he had looked in all of the places his dog Diggy liked to hide. After he called his mother for help, she looked in the same places. When Mrs. Adams, the next door neighbor, heard them calling, she began to look and call, too. Mrs. Adams told the postman about Diggy's disappearance. As the postman delivered the mail, he asked everyone he met to join in the search. Finally, the whole neighborhood was looking and calling for Diggy...

As the train roared through the night, the thunder grew louder and the lightning more fierce. Pelting rain beat against the windows. This sudden change in weather was something the tall, bearded passenger had not expected. As he shifted nervously in his chair, looking again and again at his watch, he continued to stare at the door. The other passengers were becoming increasingly aware of his nervousness. The conductor had made several trips through the car looking intently at the bearded gentleman. As the tension increased, every passenger in the car sensed that some unexpected event was about to take place...

NEWSPAPER KNOW-HOW

Class Project

LANGUAGE ARTS

Plan and produce a classroom newspaper. Involve the students in a meaningful way by making specific assignments related to topics of high interest to the students. Include news from the entire school and make sure that copies of the final product are delivered to the principal, the library, other classrooms and parents.

As preparation for the project, make available for students' perusal copies of several newspapers at least a week before the actual planning begins. Lead class discussions about what makes an interesting newspaper: length of articles, vocabulary usage, front page headlines, and overall layout. Develop a time frame and plan for the distribution. Smuggle some strong skills reinforcement into the project by reproducing and distributing copies of the editor's guide on the following page.

Suggestions for student assignments:

- an interview with the principal, school patrol person, librarian or cafeteria manager

- a sports column

- a school schedule for the upcoming month

- a listing of student honors

- a listing of new books in the library and book reviews

- a comics section

- weather forecasts

- reviews of units of study

- other topical classroom news

EDITOR'S GUIDE
LANGUAGE ARTS

Name _____

Refer to this useful editor's guide before beginning and after completing any writing project.

1. Who will read my work?

2. Will they find it interesting?

3. Have I spelled all words correctly?
    (Check any words about which you are unsure. Ask a good speller to read and check your spelling.)

4. Have I put periods, commas, question marks, exclamation points and capital letters in the right places?
    (Reread to check yourself; then, ask a friend to double-check for you.)

5. Are my ideas in the right order?
    (Did I tell the first thing first and the other things in sequence as they happened?)

6. Have I used words that my readers can understand easily?

7. Have I used interesting words that the reader will enjoy?

8. Have I used examples or illustrations to help explain my ideas?

9. Have I said what I really think, and not just what I think my friends or my teacher would expect me to say?

10. Is my ending good? Does it really end the story or idea?

11. What is special about my writing that will make readers glad that they read it?

12. What can I do to improve my writing?

SURPRISE SITUATIONS
Writing Activity
LANGUAGE ARTS

Write 20 "situations" such as the ones suggested below on strips of paper. Write the names of characters on 20 additional strips of paper. Place each set of paper strips in a plastic container labeled appropriately. Instruct each student to draw one paper strip from each container and to use the given information in a creative story.

Situations

The bus roared down the highway.

Flames shot from the ceiling
   just as someone yelled,
   "Fire!"

Characters

An old lady, her dog,
   and a siamese cat

Timi Turtle, a shy boy;
Mr. Prim, the principal;
Billy Bigshot, the class bully

DESIGN AND DESCRIBE
Creative Expression Activity
LANGUAGE ARTS

Have the students work together in teams to design a toy or sporting product that has never been manufactured. Instruct each team to draw the toy, to write a description of it, and to design the packaging for it. Then have the teams exchange papers and write advertisements for the products they receive. Share the results orally in order to determine how well the product designs were interpreted by the teams who wrote the advertisements.

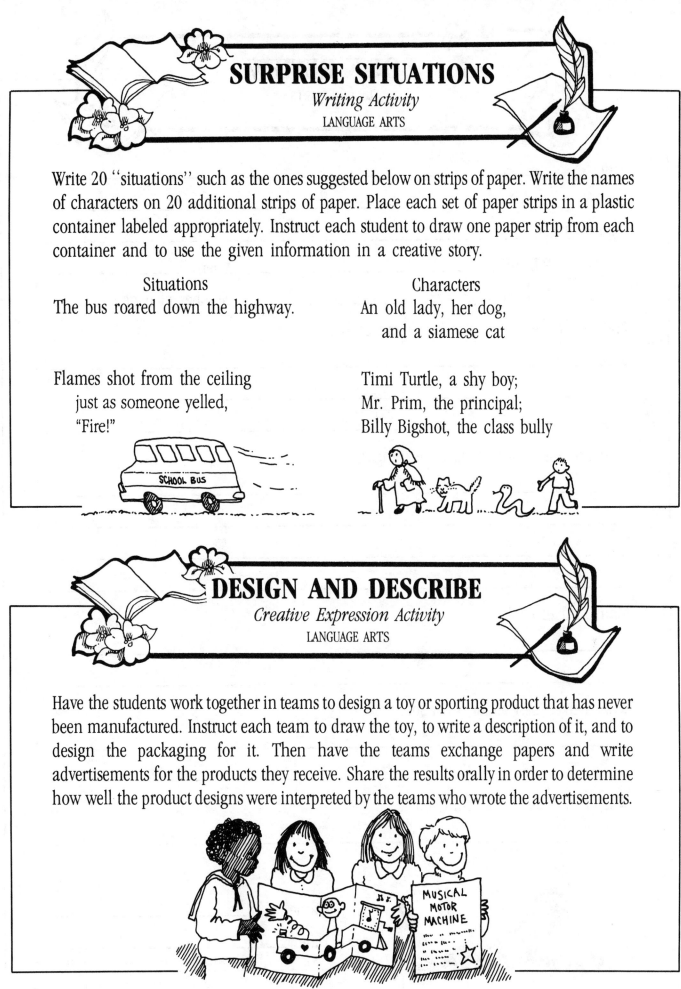

BOOK REVIEW
LANGUAGE ARTS

Title: _____

Author: _____

Published by: _____

      Where: _____   When: _____

      Type of book: _____   Number of pages: _____

Main characters (give one fact about each):

_____

_____

_____

Four interesting words (give meanings):

_____

_____

_____

_____

Main idea of book:

_____

_____

What I liked best about this book:

_____

_____

What I liked least about this book:

_____

Name _____

Date _____

MINI HOLIDAY PUZZLES
LANGUAGE ARTS

Name _____

Unscramble the Christmas words.

1. T I G F

   _ _ _ _

2. Y E M R R

   _ _ _ _ _

3. C R O D A E I T N O S

   _ _ _ _ _ _ _ _ _ _

4. T S A R

   _ _ _ _

5. A S T N A   S L A C U

   _ _ _ _ _   _ _ _ _ _

6. D E R I N E R E

   _ _ _ _ _ _ _ _

7. L E C B R E A I T N O

   _ _ _ _ _ _ _ _ _ _

8. G L E A N

   _ _ _ _ _

Find and circle 11 Halloween words.

```
f r g o b l i n b h i m
e d s p c t r e a t o z
j a c k o l a n t e r n
m g h o s p o o k w j t
o r c a t u b c a i e r
o b a m u g h o s t g i
r d o v m a s k h c a c
f m k x e b t w r h q k
```

Spooktacular words to find:

bat	mask	cat	witch
spook	costume	treat	jack-o'-lantern
ghost	trick	goblin	

Color by symbol to find a Thanksgiving surprise.

orange 🍂 brown 🍁
red ❤ green ❧

Find and circle 4 elves hiding in the picture.

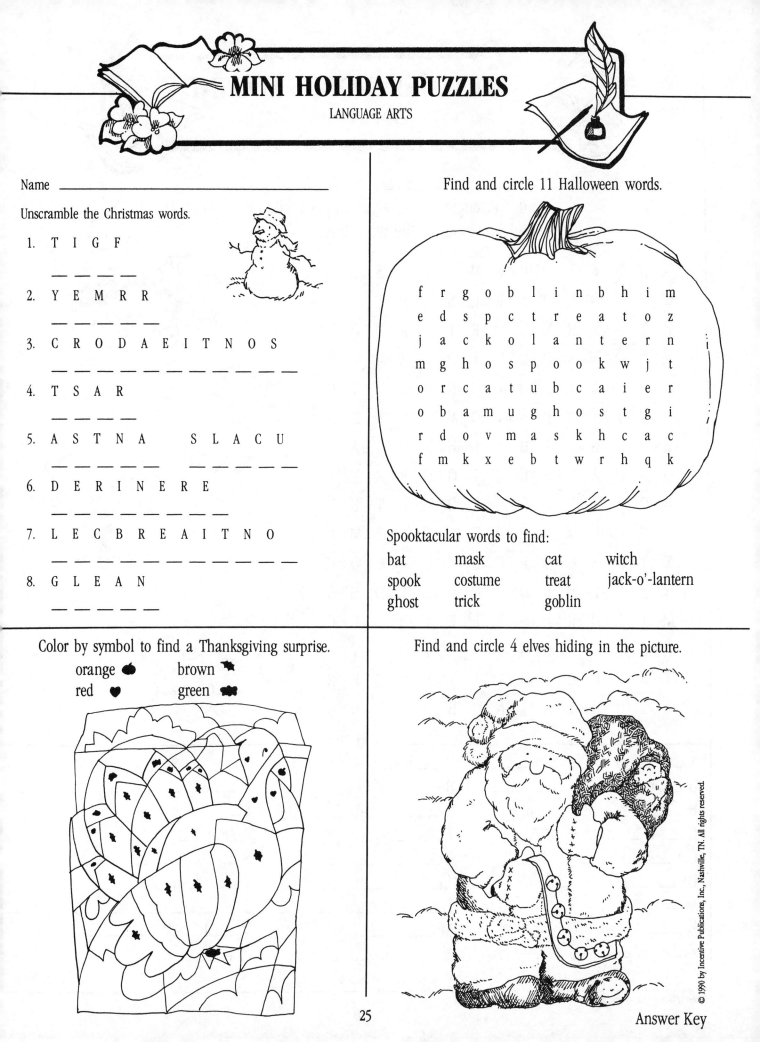

25

Answer Key

WEATHER WORDS TO FIND

LANGUAGE ARTS

Name _____

Find and circle twenty-eight words related to weather.
Write the words in the word box.

```
A K D F I O C U M U L U S S N
W I C D H P L E C S A P E N I
K T H E R M O M E T E R V O M
M N Q W A D U B I O L E B W B
V C H A I L D L O R H S M I U
E R I X N R S I O M G S E D S
L F O G J T B Z L B H U Y A C
O R U A O H K Z J O U R X N I
C O I I F U B A R O M E T E R
I S C L M N Z R U L I C E M R
T T I S G D P D G A D W C O U
Y R C L M E D Z O Y I I D M S
M I L D R R S L E E T N Z E C
H S E G A O S U N N Y D E T F
T A W B C T D V I J L A S E R
L I G H T N I N G B O U P R E
```

Word Box

A _ _ m _ _ _ _ t _ _   G _ i _   S _ _ w

B _ r _ m _ _ _ _ _   H _ _ l   S _ _ e e _

B _ _ z _ _ _ d   H _ m _ d _ _ _   S _ n _ y

C _ r _ u _   I _ _   R _ i _

C l _ _ _ _ _ _   I _ i _ _ _ _   S _ _ _ _

C _ _ u l _ _   L _ s e _   T _ _ n _ _ _

D _ _ _   L _ g _ _ n _ _ _   T h _ _ _ _ o _ _ _ _ e

F _ _ _   M _ l _ _   V _ l _ c _ _ _ _

F _ _ _ s _   N _ m b _ _ _   Wi _ _ _

                          P _ _ _ s _ _ _ r _

Answer Key

© 1990 by Incentive Publications, Inc., Nashville, TN. All rights reserved.

26

EXCUSE THE EXAGGERATING

Vocabulary Development

LANGUAGE ARTS

Stretch vocabularies and encourage creative thinking by engaging students in an oral discussion of exaggerations, leading into the development of the most exaggerated exaggerations they can think of.

Begin by presenting a very simple sentence and asking the students to help turn it into an exaggerated exaggeration.

> Example: "The boy yelled loudly."
> "The boy yelled so loudly he scared his whole family."
> "The boy yelled loudly enough to annoy all the neighbors."
> "The boy yelled loudly enough to disturb the whole town."

When the students agree that all possibilities have been exhausted for "stretching the exaggeration," write the last sentence on the board.

Continue the activity (allowing students to supply the beginning sentence) until at least ten or twelve "exaggerated exaggerations" have been written on the board.

Provide paper and pencils, and ask students to select one of the exaggerations to use as the basis for a tall tale. Provide time for completed stories to be read aloud to the group.

Variation: Provide drawing paper and crayons, and ask students to select an "exaggerated exaggeration" to illustrate.

FAMILY HISTORIES
Writing Activity
LANGUAGE ARTS

Have students write their own family histories. Assist them in first making a list of important names, dates, significant events and any interesting facts or stories handed down from generation to generation.

They may use this list to develop an outline from which the history will be written.

This activity will provide meaningful practice in organizing and using real facts to develop an  original composition. The completed composition will also enhance the students' sense of self-worth and family pride.

FLYING HIGH
Group Game/Listening
LANGUAGE ARTS

Appoint one student as the leader, and ask the rest of the students to attempt to follow the directions given. When the leader names something that flies, the followers are to flap their arms as if they were wings.

Example: "Sparrows fly."   "Crows fly."
                "Helicopters fly."   "Kites fly."
                "Bats fly."

If the leader says, "Cars flys, cows fly, boys fly, houses fly," followers who flap their wings are out of the game. The last person left in is declared the winner and becomes the next leader. Good leaders try to trick followers by "flapping their wings" when calling things that do not fly.

BUILD A STORY
Individual Activity/Reading
LANGUAGE ARTS

Cut short stories from magazines, newspapers or old textbooks (or write your own). Cut the stories into several sections and place in a folder or envelope with the story title printed on the front. Enclose a worksheet comparable to the following (several worksheets may be included in one envelope with directions asking students to return story sections when finished and replacing the envelope for the next student's use).

Name _____

Read the story sections and arrange them in the correct order to tell the story. Then complete these sentences:

This story is about _____.

It happened _____ _____.

Another way it could have ended is _____ _____ _____ .

STORY CUTUPS
Group Activity/Sequencing
LANGUAGE ARTS

Cut stories from old readers, story books or magazines. Separate the paragraphs and place the parts for each story in an envelope.

Provide envelopes, sheets of construction paper and glue so the stories may be reconstructed on new pages. Ask students to give their own titles to the stories.

When the stories are together, provide time for students to read their stories aloud in a small group setting for discussion and to see if their classmates think the titles "fit."

Variations: If pictures are available with the stories, include them in the envelope. Students will enjoy trying to fit the pictures with the correct paragraphs.

For advanced students, combining all the parts of two or three stories in one envelope would make the activity more difficult as well as provide an experience in fitting together related ideas.

PRESENT A PLAY
Group Drama Activity
LANGUAGE ARTS

Surprise your students one morning by telling them that today will be "play day." Scheduled assignments will be limited to the "barest essentials," and the rest of the day will be dedicated to planning and presenting plays.

Begin by asking students to number off in groups of five or six (depending on the class size). All the ones become one group, the twos another group, etc. Each group then meets to decide on a story topic or theme and to plan their plays.

Explain that they may use any form they choose (puppets, TV show, traditional performances with each student having a speaking part, pantomime, a musical, etc.) and any materials available for props and costumes. The only restrictions are a specified time limit for the performance, and all group members must participate in the project.

Themes selected may range from fairy tales and fables to reinactment of a historical event or satirical situations based on community or school culture.

Less mature children may select old favorite stories or nursery rhymes. The entire class including the teacher will most likely be surprised at the wide range of spontaneity and creativity displayed in the selection of topics and material utilization. Everything from personal jewelry, lunch money, scarves and sweaters to school tools and plants may be utilized in the presentations.

The culmination of the day will be the presentations themselves! Everyone will go home a bit richer for the memory-making day, and chances are good that any basic skills not covered during the day will be approached with renewed zeal on the next day.

TEACHABLE MOMENTS
Games

LANGUAGE ARTS

Sometimes the most "teachable moments" come at the most unexpected times. Three old favorite, never-fail activities to help make use of these valuable times are:

SENTENCE OR PHRASE OF THE DAY

Write a key sentence or phrase from a well-known book of fiction, poetry or special subject area book on the board each morning. The first student to identify the book and author by writing it on the board wins the privilege of selecting the next sentence or phrase.

WORD USAGE

Early in the day, discuss cliches with the students and list on the board familiar cliches supplied by the students. Ask the students to carry a pad and pencil with them and jot down every single cliche they either read or hear. At the end of the day, provide time for students to compare and share their lists. This adds a spark of interest to the day as well as providing a sharp focus on both the spoken and written word.

WRITING/IDENTIFYING AUTHOR'S STYLE

Write a paragraph on the chalkboard or a chart and ask the students to analyze it from the standpoint of the writer's style. Does the writer use short or long single or complex sentences, descriptive words and phrases, sensationalism, a negative or positive approach to the subject, etc., to capture the reader's attention? This activity will serve a twofold purpose. As students become increasingly aware of one individual author's style, they will at the same time be able to compare and contrast the work of various authors.

SCIENCE

SENSATIONAL SENSES
Sensory Exploration
SCIENCE

Use this fun activity to stimulate students' awareness of the functions of the five senses. Place objects on a table to be categorized by smell, taste, touch, sound or sight. (Small: onion, potpourri; Taste: sugar, salt, orange and apple slices; Touch: silk, sandpaper, bark, leather; Sound: bell, whistle, alarm clock; Sight: book, flashlight, picture.) Ask the students to select an item from the table and to tell which of the five senses would be most responsive to the item. Include activities such as these:

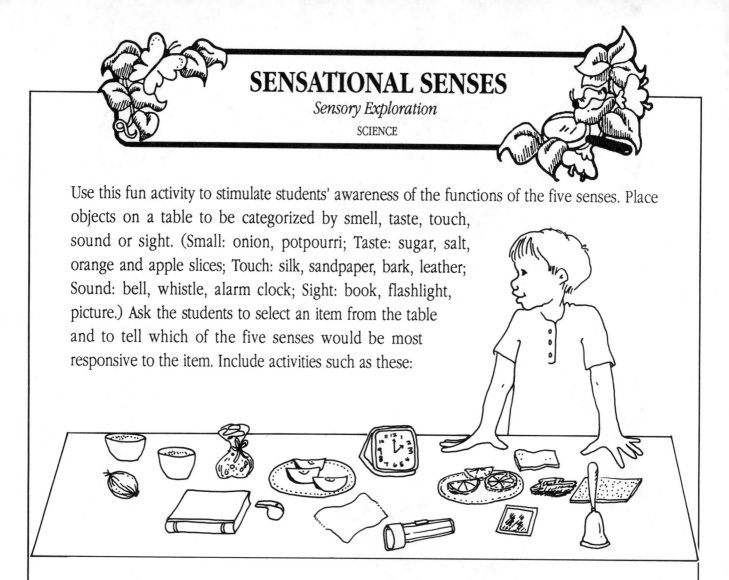

1. If you and a friend were locked in the school on a dark night, would you rather have a flashlight or a whistle? Why?

2. If you could choose a rose or a bag of jellybeans as a present for your teachers, which would you choose and why?

3. If you were going on a trip in a car, would you rather have a favorite book or a tape player and a favorite tape? Why?

MY FIVE SENSES

Self-Awareness/Construction Activity

SCIENCE

The sensory activity will get students "personally involved." Have the students make "My Five Senses" booklets. Direct the students to write and complete each sentence below on a sheet of drawing paper. Then have students look through magazines and catalogs to find and cut out pictures of things they like to touch, see, hear, smell and taste. Instruct the students to paste each picture on the appropriate "senses" page. Collage covers can be made by pasting pictures of things that can be touched, seen, heard, smelled and tasted on a colorful piece of construction paper. Punch holes in the pages and tie them together with yarn to make individual booklets. Display the finished products on a table for all to read!

I am glad that I have taste buds because _____ .

I think my nose is _____ .

One thing about my ears is _____ .

My eyes are _____ .

A warm hug makes me feel _____ .

LOOK! LOOK!
Eye Investigations
SCIENCE

Give each student a small mirror. Tell the students to hold the mirrors close to them so that they can see only their eyes. Ask these questions and discuss the responses:

1. What do you see in the mirror?
2. What color are your eyes?
3. What do you see over your eyes?
4. Why do you think we have eyebrows and eyelashes?
5. What would happen to our eyes if we had no eyelashes?
6. Of what are eyelids made?
7. How are eyelids like window shades?
8. How do eyelids protect our eyes?
9. Why are eyes shy?
10. What makes tears?
11. What is the black spot in the middle of the eye called?

Explain how the pupil works (when the eye needs a lot of light, the pupil gets big; when the eye needs a little light, the pupil gets small). Have students partially close their eyes, keeping them open just a little bit so that they can barely see. Count to ten and then ask the students to open their eyes very wide. Instruct each student to watch one pupil in the mirror. Discuss what happens.

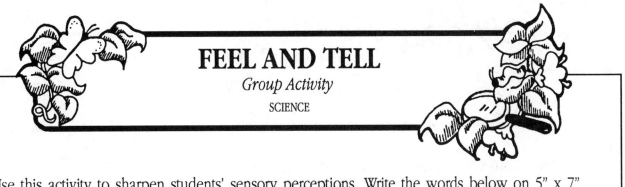

FEEL AND TELL
Group Activity
SCIENCE

Use this activity to sharpen students' sensory perceptions. Write the words below on 5" x 7" index cards.

smooth	slimy	scratchy	squishy	grainy	woolly
hard	soft	rough	waxy	slick	crumbly

Place a variety of familiar objects with distinctive textures and shapes in a shopping bag (pencil, rock, sandpaper, spoon, feather, sock, etc.). Ask one student at a time to reach into the bag and pick up an object. Without looking at the object, the student should describe it as fully as possible. Encourage students to speak in complete sentences and to use interesting, descriptive words. After everyone has had a turn, place the objects on a table. Hand out the word cards and ask each student to select an item from the table that can be described by the descriptive word. Each student should describe the item by using the descriptive word in a complete sentence and then name other objects that have the same quality.

EXPERIMENT WITH A FLASHLIGHT
Color Experiment
SCIENCE

Cover one flashlight with red cellophane, another with blue cellophane, and a third with green cellophane. Let students experiment with color by shining each flashlight on a white wall, a sheet attached to a wall, or a screen. Ask two students to shine the red and green flashlights on the same spot. Have pairs of students repeat this experiment with various color combinations to find out how primary colors can be combined to form secondary colors. Before putting away the flashlights, allow the students to enjoy "flashing" in time to music or improvising a rain dance or jungle animal parade.

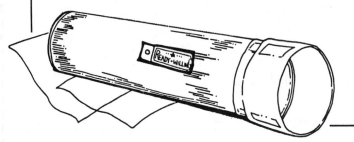

SMELL WELL
Sense of Smell
SCIENCE

Discuss the process of smelling. Ask the students if they can smell by taking air in through their mouths. Conduct this simple experiment to help the students answer the question.

Place an onion, a bar of soap, or a lemon on a table. Ask one student at a time to come to the table and to hold the object in front of his nose (with mouth closed). Then tell the student to breathe in through the nose. Next have the student hold his nose while holding the object in front of his mouth. Ask the student which time he was able to smell the object.

A TASTING PARTY
Taste Identification Experiment
SCIENCE

Put foods such as lemons, dill pickles, uncooked oatmeal, salt, ketchup, cocoa, sugar, etc., in separate containers. Place the containers on a table. Let small groups of students go to the table. Have a student close his eyes and then "feed" the student a small sample of each food. Ask the student to identify each food. After every student has had a turn, discuss the accuracy of the guesses and any problems the students might have had in identifying the foods.

1. Waxed paper milk cartons (1/2 gallon, 1 quart, 1 pint and 1/2 pint)

   For measuring, building birdhouses and feeders, holding collections, and potting plants

2. Plastic bleach, juice and milk jugs

   For measuring, conducting experiments, watering plants, and making puddle scoops

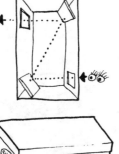

3. Shoe boxes of all sizes

   For holding collections, making peep boxes, dioramas, individual science tool kits, and periscopes

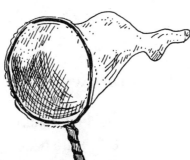

4. Nylon hosiery

   For making insect catchers and fishnets and for use as tops of insect cages

5. Six-pack soft drink containers

   For holding science tools and collections

6. Glass jars with tops (1 gallon, 1/2 gallon, 1 quart, 1 pint and 1/2 pint)

    For making terrariums, aquariums, and vivariums and for holding water for experiments

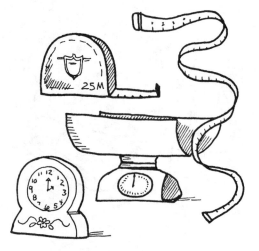

7. Metric and standard measuring tapes
    Scales
    Old but workable alarm clock

    For general use in measuring lengths, widths, heights and time

8. Plastic food containers

    For potting plants and temporarily housing insects or snails (nylon hose secured over the top of the container with a rubber band)

9. Freezer bags

    For holding collections and for making project "starter kits"

10. Magnets of all sizes and shapes
    For experiments

11. String, rubber bands, fishing line and yarn

    For experiments, student-made books and miscellaneous projects

12. Small blocks of scrap lumber, wood shavings, corrugated cardboard, sawdust and styrofoam pieces

    For experiments and miscellaneous uses

13. Plastic eggs (e.g. the kind that contains hosiery)

    For holding collections, games, instructions and materials for experiments

14. Cardboard tubes, mailing tubes or tissue and paper towel rolls

    For holding posters and art projects and for use in experiments and construction projects

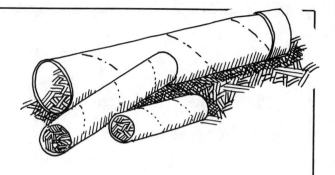

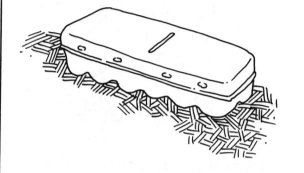

15. Egg cartons

    For categorizing objects, sorting and storing collections (seeds, shells, stones, magnets, screws, etc.), and for planting seeds

16. Coffee, shortening and potato chip cans

    For holding potting soil, collections and art supplies, or for use as a game or portable minicenter container

17. Greeting card or stationery boxes (especially ones with clear plastic tops)

    For holding collections, card games, and mini jigsaw puzzles

18. Collection of small stones

    For categorizing activities, construction projects, and for use as counters and game parts

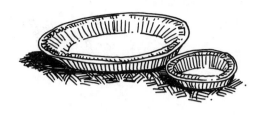

19. Aluminum pie pans

    For holding collections and for use in experiments

20. Nails, screws and washers

    For use in categorizing activities, experiments and miscellaneous projects

21. Plastic eating utensils and small plastic pails

    For use in games and experiments (storage, stirring and spreading)

22. Clean sand stored in plastic or glass jars

    For terrariums, aquariums, experiments and art projects

23. Baskets and shopping bags

    For collecting and storing supplies, games, and minicenters (especially good for projects or supplies that need to be carried from one place to another)

LET OFF A LITTLE STEAM!
Experiment
SCIENCE

Have the class watch as you place a tray of water in the freezer. Ask the students to discuss what they think will happen. The next day, let the students examine the tray and feel the ice cubes. Discuss what happened. Place the ice in a pan and put the pan on a hot plate. When the ice has melted, bring the water to a boil. Talk about how steam is formed. Hold a piece of paper over the steam and let each student touch the paper and tell how it feels.

OIL AND WATER DO NOT MIX
Experiment
SCIENCE

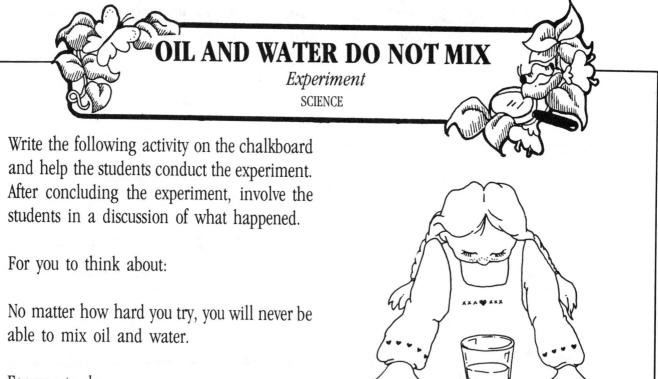

Write the following activity on the chalkboard and help the students conduct the experiment. After concluding the experiment, involve the students in a discussion of what happened.

For you to think about:

No matter how hard you try, you will never be able to mix oil and water.

For you to do:
1. Fill a glass with water. Add a spoonful of oil.
2. Stir the liquid until the oil breaks up into drops.
3. Stop stirring and watch the oil rise to the top of the water.

ANIMAL ANTHOLOGY
Art Project
SCIENCE

Make a list of animals from A to Z. Ask each student to use Manila paper, crayons and markers to illustrate one or more of the animals so that every letter of the alphabet is represented. Allow the students to use resource books for help in drawing details and distinguishing features. When the drawings have been completed, have each student write the name of the animal(s) and one short sentence about the animal(s) below the illustration(s). Staple the pages together to make a book and add an attractive cover. Make a class trip to another class to present the book, or invite the class to your room to receive the book. The visit also could include a brief skit, a simple game and

refreshments. This activity makes a good culminating project for a study of animals.

DYED TO ORDER
Natural Dyes Experiment
SCIENCE

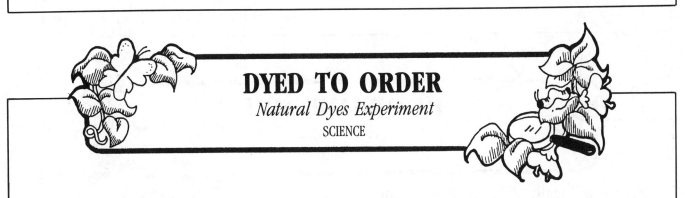

Collect natural materials such as pokeberries, onions, elderberries, leaves, roots, bark,

carrots, beets, rose petals, etc., and seep them in water to make dyes. Experiment to see what colors and color variations can be obtained. Ask the students to dip pieces of muslin or other natural materials in the dyes. Tie dyeing and/or cutting the fabric into unusual shapes and mounting them on construction paper backgrounds will add interest. Arrange an attractive bulletin board displaying the results.

STUDY ROCKS!
Inquiry Activity
SCIENCE

Place a collection of different kinds of rocks on the science table. Students might enjoy contributing to the collection. Use the rocks for these activities:

1. Rank-order the rocks:
    lightest to heaviest
    largest to smallest
    lightest color to darkest color
    dullest to shiniest
    smoothest to roughest
2. Classify the rocks according to size, shape, type, etc., by separating them into egg cartons or muffin tins.
3. Make a list of descriptive words for each rock.
4. Make a list of uses for rocks.
5. Name ten things made from rocks.
6. Make pet rocks! (Do this as a final activity.) Use buttons, yarn, colorful paper, paint, paste and whatever materials you choose to make faces and features. Use a box to make a home for the pet rock.

HOMEMADE SOIL
Experiment
SCIENCE

Students will really take interest in this unusual experiment. Place some "crumbly" rocks (such as shale and sandstone) on top of a large, flat rock and cover the rocks with a cloth. Let the students take turns hitting the rocks with a hammer. Brush the tiny rock pieces into a flowerpot (one with a hole in the bottom). Help the students water the soil mixture and plant bean seeds. Make sure the students keep the soil damp but not soggy. Observe to see what happens! (Although this homemade soil does not contain enough food to support a plant for a long period, a seedling probably will sprout.)

TALK ON A TIN CAN PHONE

Construction Activity/Game

SCIENCE

Help the students construct make-believe telephones. Wash and dry two tin cans for every student. Use a nail to carefully punch a hole in the bottom of each can. Have each student thread four to six feet of string through the hole in each can and tie knots on the insides of the cans. Let the students play this game.

Divide the class into teams. Each team must select a "caller" and a "receiver." The caller stands with his back to the team and holds a can to his mouth. The receiver faces the caller, holding the other can to his ear. Upon hearing the word "go," the caller says the name of a team member and the receiver runs to tag that person. The person whose name was called must run to grab the phone before a member of the other team does. The receiver then becomes the caller and the person whose name was called becomes the receiver. The team with the most people to grab the phone first wins.

FROM ANOTHER POINT OF VIEW

Construction/Experimentation Activity

SCIENCE

FOLD ON DOTTED LINES.

Make a periscope for the science table. You will need two pocket mirrors (2" x 3"), sturdy construction paper and glue. Fold the construction paper as directed by the pattern. (You may need to scale the pattern up or down to fit the size of available mirrors.) Insert the mirrors so that each rests at a 45° angle and glue them in place. Let the students enjoy experimenting with the periscope and viewing the world from a new "point of view"!

12" x 18"

SCIENTIFICALLY SPEAKING

SCIENCE

Name _____

Use resource books to help you find one-line definitions for the following terms.
Write each definition on the line below the term.

1. Hypothesis

    _____

2. Odometer

    _____

3. Mammal

    _____

4. Camouflage

    _____

5. Endangered Species

    _____

6. Algae

    _____

7. Invertebrate

    _____

8. Spelunker

    _____

9. Cardiovascular

    _____

10. Galaxy

    _____

11. Molecule

    _____

12. Fungi

    _____

13. Archaeologist

    _____

14. Paleontologist

    _____

15. Photosynthesis

    _____

16. Amphibian

    _____

TAKE A LISTENING WALK
Outdoor Excursion
SCIENCE

Take the class on a listening walk! Walk around the school grounds or through the immediate neighborhood. Ask the students to be very quiet and to listen for every sound as they walk. Have the students count the sounds made by animals, machines and the wind. Discuss the sounds heard on the walk after returning to the classroom.

MUSICAL BOTTLES
Tone Experiment
SCIENCE

Fill several pop bottles with different amounts of water. Fill one bottle 3/4 full and leave one bottle empty. Let the students take turns blowing across the tops of the bottles to make tones. Ask these questions:

Which bottle makes the highest tone?
Which bottle makes the lowest tone?
What effect does the amount of air (or water) in the bottle have on the sound produced?

EASY INSTRUMENTS
Construction Activity
SCIENCE

Help the students make simple instruments to use in experimenting with sound!

Sandpaper Shufflers

Glue sandpaper on one side of each of two blocks of wood. Rub the sandpaper surfaces together to make sounds.

Tambourine

Attach several small bells to the rim of a heavy paper plate. Decorate the plate with crayons or markers if desired. Shake, shake, shake!

Drums

Turn round cardboard cartons or tin cans into drums. Pencils (that have not been sharpened) with big erasers make great drumsticks!

Sound Boxes

Fill small boxes, cottage cheese containers or ice cream cartons with "sound-making" items such as marbles, rice, dried beans, pebbles or sand. Secure the top or lid. Shake or beat to make lots of noise!

Humbuzzer

Punch several holes around a cardboard tube about 1 1/2 inches from one end. Place a square of wax paper (2" longer than the diameter of the tube) over the end in which holes have been punched. Secure the wax paper with a rubber band. Hold the humbuzzer against your mouth and hum through the wax paper to make buzzing noise.

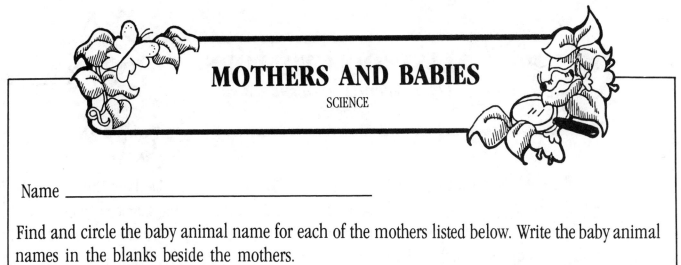

MOTHERS AND BABIES

SCIENCE

Name _____

Find and circle the baby animal name for each of the mothers listed below. Write the baby animal names in the blanks beside the mothers.

```
D  U  C  K  L  I  N  G
I  C  A  I  X  E  N  O
K  H  L  T  Q  W  W  S
S  I  F  T  B  M  A  L
R  C  L  E  U  R  F  I
M  K  A  N  C  S  M  N
P  I  G  L  E  T  E  G
```

goose   _ _ _ _ _ _ _

lioness _ _ _

doe   _ _ _ _

sow   _ _ _ _ _ _

hen   _ _ _ _ _ _

nanny   _ _ _

duck   _ _ _ _ _ _ _

ewe   _ _ _ _

heifer   _ _ _ _ _

cat   _ _ _ _ _ _

Answer Key

CLASSROOM VISITORS
Construction/Observation Activity

SCIENCE

Bring the outdoors inside — for a brief stay only! Help students make these simple "homes" for temporary classroom guests. Keep the containers in the science center and make sure that students check them daily for food and water. (Never place the containers in direct sunlight!) Return the animals to their natural environment after one week.

Aquarium

Put a layer of mud in the bottom of a gallon jar. Bed water plants in the mud and cover the mud with ½" of clean sand. Fill the jar with pond water, rain water or tap water (let tap water stand overnight). Stock the aquarium with minnows, snails and polywogs.

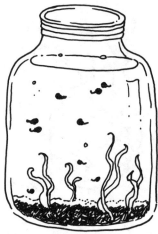

Terrarium

Lay a gallon jar on its side and place it in a stand made from a box top. Put a quart of damp soil, a wet piece of wood, and small, moss-covered rocks in the jar. Place a bottle cap or jar lid in the jar and keep it filled with water. Punch holes in the lid (flatten edges around the holes so that animals will not get hurt). Frogs, toads, salamanders, snails and millipedes are perfect guests for this home! Feed them lettuce, flower petals, raw hamburger, dry bread and dead insects.

Bug Home

Cut windows in two sides of a half-gallon milk carton. Slip a nylon stocking over the entire carton and knot it at the top. Beetles, spiders and other bugs will need water at all times. Some beetles will eat leaves, bits of hamburger, or bread. Spiders will eat tiny mealworms, ants or any live insect dropped into the web. Caterpillars and grasshoppers need the leaves and grass blades they are living on to supply them with food and water.

SNAIL OBSERVATORY
Observation Experiment
SCIENCE

Snails make very interesting classroom guests. Let the students help make a home for a snail who will be the "classroom guest" for one week.

Fill the bottom of a quart jar with soil. Place a lettuce leaf and a small jar filled with a teaspoon of water in the container. (This is enough food for one week.)

Take the class on a snail hunt in an empty lot or nearby garden. Carefully transport the snail to its new home. Lead an observation/discovery session by giving the following instructions and asking related questions. Encourage the students to contribute to the discussion.

1. Watch the snail move.
    Can you see the snail's foot?
    What happens to the grass as the snail moves over it?
    (The snail's foot produces a wet substance which helps him move.)

2. Try to find the snail's eyes.
    How would you like to have eyes on the ends of stalks and be able to see in all directions at once?

3. Touch the snail's head very gently.
    What does the snail do?
    (The snail uses the shorter stalks for smelling and feeling.)

4. Touch the snail's shell.
    Do you think the snail is attached to the shell?

THE A-B-C'S OF BIRDS
Poster Construction
SCIENCE

Have the class make an A-B-C bird poster! Ask the students to find a bird name for each letter of the alphabet. Let the students illustrate the birds or find pictures of the birds in old magazines to glue on the poster.

WHAT BIRD AM I?
Riddles
SCIENCE

Ask the students to write bird riddles for friends to answer. For example: I am a showy redbird often seen in hedges and shrubs (cardinal). Have the students print the riddles on strips of paper. Staple the paper together to make a bird riddle book for the reading table.

TAKE A BIRD WALK
Field Trip
SCIENCE

Plan a "bird walk" to develop students' curiosity about the knowledge of the origins and habits of birds. Let the students help plan the trip. It may be as simple as a walk around the school grounds or as elaborate as a trip to the natural wildlife museum. Allow time before the trip for students to look through resource books containing pictures of and information about birds. Tell the students to find out as much as they can about birds. Then ask the students to help you make a list of "things to find out" about birds. (Write the list on the board.) After the trip, lead a follow-up discussion based on the "things to find out" list. Make a list of the observations made and the facts gained.

BIRDS HAVE, OR BIRDS HAVE NOT
Dot-To-Dot Puzzle
SCIENCE

Enlarge this simple dot-to-dot puzzle to make a pupil activity sheet. Write the following instructions on the page:

Follow the directions to find a fine bird!

Draw a line from:

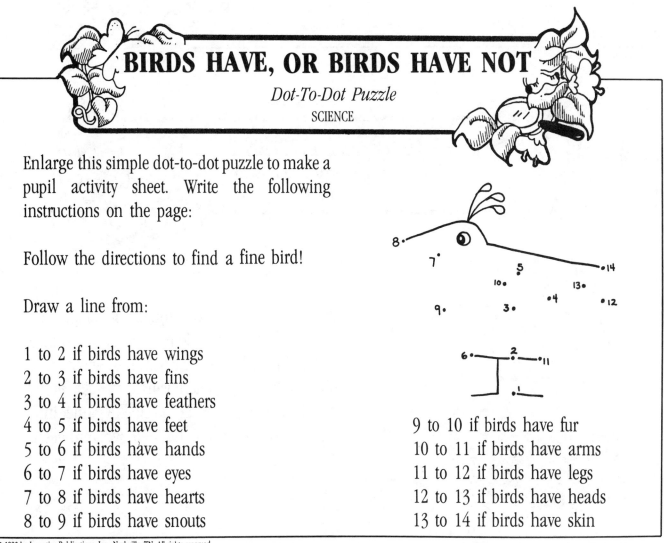

1 to 2 if birds have wings
2 to 3 if birds have fins
3 to 4 if birds have feathers
4 to 5 if birds have feet
5 to 6 if birds have hands
6 to 7 if birds have eyes
7 to 8 if birds have hearts
8 to 9 if birds have snouts

9 to 10 if birds have fur
10 to 11 if birds have arms
11 to 12 if birds have legs
12 to 13 if birds have heads
13 to 14 if birds have skin

BIRDS CAN BE PUZZLING
Jigsaw Puzzles
SCIENCE

Let the students make bird puzzles! Have the students paste large, colorful pictures of birds on tagboard. Instruct the students to cut the pictures apart to make jigsaw puzzles. Students will enjoy trading and working the puzzles as a free-time activity.

INSPECT A NEST
Inspection/Construction Activity
SCIENCE

Place a bird's nest (one that's not being used) on a table for the students to inspect and take apart in order to learn more about nest building and the materials used to make nests. Allow the students to go outside to gather bird nest materials for making their own bird nests.

BIRD WORDS TO FIND
Chalkboard Activity Or Pupil Worksheet
SCIENCE

Write this activity on the chalkboard or use it for a pupil worksheet. Have one student at a time go to the board and read a sentence. The student must find and circle the word in the puzzle and then write the word in the blanks to complete the sentence.

```
B  J  D  O  W  L  S  F
C  A  R  D  I  N  A  L
E  Y  B  E  R  E  D  Y
G  H  E  G  G  S  A  P
F  L  S  O  U  T  H  C
V  W  O  R  M  S  O  I
```

1. The wise old __ __ __ goes whoo-whoo.
2. The __ __ __ __ __ __ __ __ is a bright red bird.
3. The blue __ __ __ is a noisy bird.
4. Birds are hatched from __ __ __ __ .
5. Mother birds teach baby birds to __ __ __ .
6. Mother birds feed __ __ __ __ __ to their babies.
7. Mother birds build __ __ __ __ __ for their eggs.
8. Many birds fly __ __ __ __ __ for the winter.

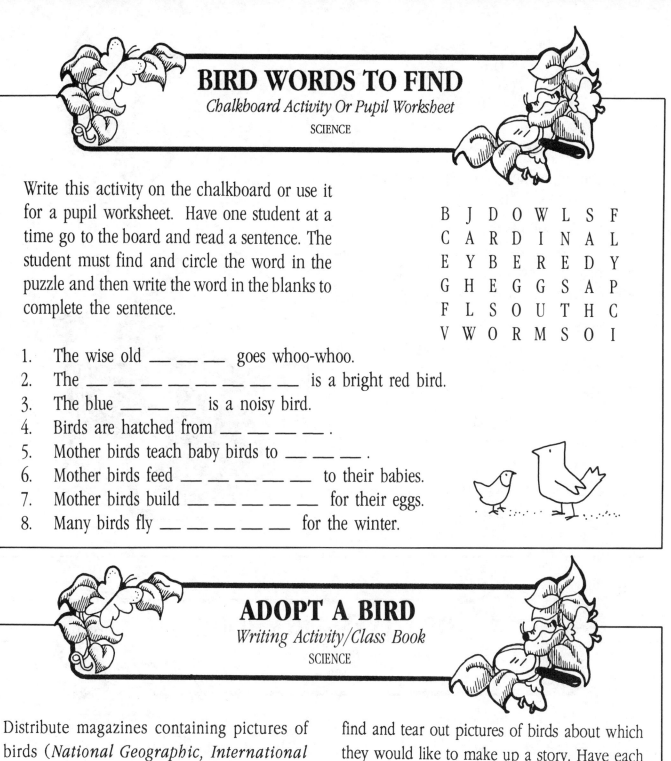

ADOPT A BIRD
Writing Activity/Class Book
SCIENCE

Distribute magazines containing pictures of birds (*National Geographic, International Wildlife,* etc.) to the students. Have students find and tear out pictures of birds about which they would like to make up a story. Have each student write a very brief story at the bottom of a sheet of drawing paper and paste the bird picture above it. Allow the students to take turns telling their stories to the class. Collect the stories, punch holes in them, and bind them together with yarn. Involve the students in designing a cover for the class book. Place the book on the reading table or in a science center.

Answer Key

BIRDS CAN BE TRICKY
Chart Activity Or Pupil Worksheet
SCIENCE

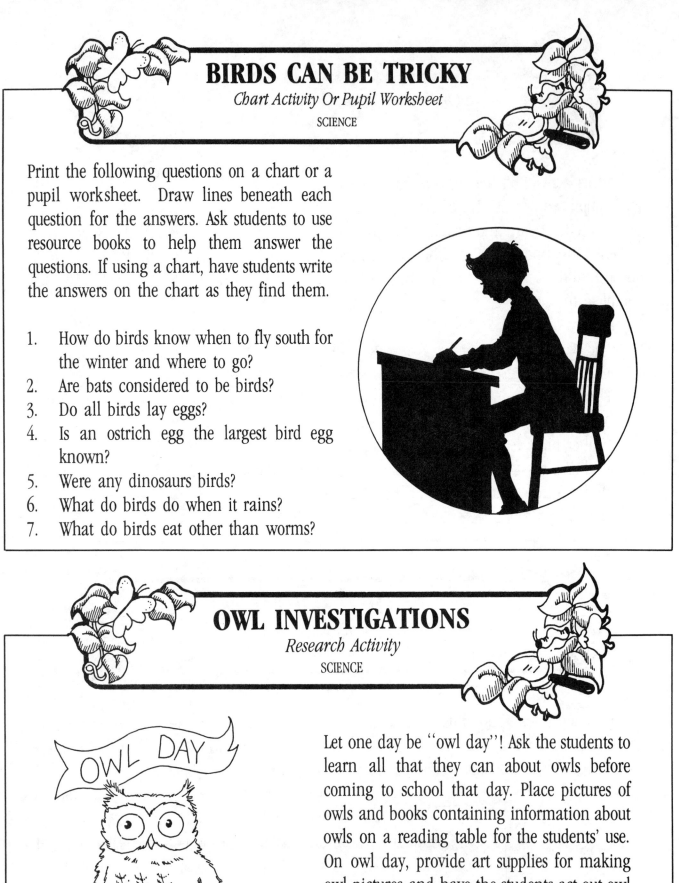

Print the following questions on a chart or a pupil worksheet. Draw lines beneath each question for the answers. Ask students to use resource books to help them answer the questions. If using a chart, have students write the answers on the chart as they find them.

1. How do birds know when to fly south for the winter and where to go?
2. Are bats considered to be birds?
3. Do all birds lay eggs?
4. Is an ostrich egg the largest bird egg known?
5. Were any dinosaurs birds?
6. What do birds do when it rains?
7. What do birds eat other than worms?

OWL INVESTIGATIONS
Research Activity
SCIENCE

OWL DAY

Let one day be "owl day"! Ask the students to learn all that they can about owls before coming to school that day. Place pictures of owls and books containing information about owls on a reading table for the students' use. On owl day, provide art supplies for making owl pictures and have the students act out owl poses. Allow students to present "owl facts" during the day. Before time to leave, list on a chart all of the facts presented that day.

BIRD FEEDERS TO MAKE
Construction/Writing Activity
SCIENCE

Help the students make bird feeders! Hang the feeders outside and observe them daily. Have the students write experience stories about what happens. If nothing happens, have the students write about that!

1. Dab peanut butter on pinecones. Place the pinecones in a shrub or hang them from low tree branches.

2. Ask students to bring empty milk cartons from home. Cut a "window" in the front of a milk carton. Close the top front of the carton and tape or glue it shut. Roll a piece of suet in birdseed and place it in the feeder. Make a hole in the top and pull a piece of cord through the hole to use in hanging the feeder.

3. Thread a needle with a long length of thread. String pieces of fruit and small pieces of fat on the thread, leaving room between each piece to tie on ribbon or yarn bows (to help attract the birds' attention). Loop the garland over a tree branch or shrub.

GROW SEED, GROW!
Creative Expression
SCIENCE

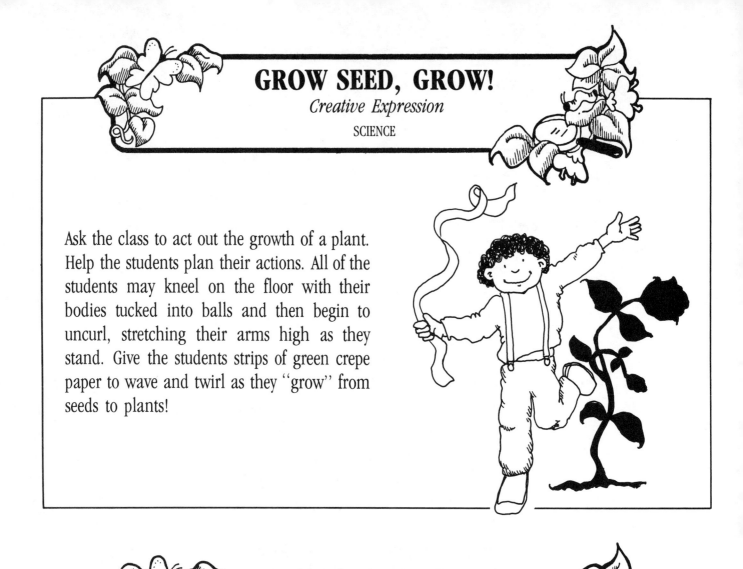

Ask the class to act out the growth of a plant. Help the students plan their actions. All of the students may kneel on the floor with their bodies tucked into balls and then begin to uncurl, stretching their arms high as they stand. Give the students strips of green crepe paper to wave and twirl as they "grow" from seeds to plants!

PLANT PROPAGATION
Demonstration
SCIENCE

Plan and present a plant propagation demonstration for the class. Show the students how plants may be started from seeds, root cuttings and bulbs. Display resource books with pictures as well as posters (made by you) and pictures for visual aids. Conclude the demonstration by allowing the students to help plant seeds, bulbs and root cuttings in several pots. Place the pots in a sunny window and water them regularly. Students will enjoy watching the new plants grow!

DIFFERENT BEGINNINGS

SCIENCE

Label each plant according to how it is started:

cutting   bulb   seed

Name _____

Date _____

A GUIDE
FOR OBSERVING A PLANT
SCIENCE

Name of plant: _____

Look carefully at the plant.
Draw a sketch of the plant in the box below.
Label the main parts of the plant in the chart.

		Color	Shape	Size	Texture
	Flower				
	Leaves				
	Stem				
Sketch of Plant	Root				

Did the plant grow from ☐ a seed   ☐ a bulb   ☐ another plant?

If any part of the plant has a distinct odor, name that part: _____

If any part of the plant is used for food by human beings, check the name of the part:

☐ stem   ☐ root   ☐ seed   ☐ fruit   ☐ flower   ☐ leaf

Are the seeds of the plant ☐ large or ☐ small?

Other observations:

_____

_____

_____

Name _____   Date _____

WATCH A SALAD GROW

SCIENCE

Name _____

1. Fill a clear plastic cup with soil.
2. Plant two or three lettuce, radish or parsley seeds.
3. Water the soil.
4. Observe to find out how long it takes for the seeds to sprout.
5. Remove all but the strongest plant.
6. Draw pictures and add dates to complete the chart below.

Seeds planted on _____ _____ .	Seeds observed on _____ _____ .	Green showing on _____ _____ .
Plants removed on _____ _____ .	This is how the plant looked on _____ .	This is what happened on _____ .

MATH

CREATE A THINK TANK!

Free-time Activity

MATH

Fill a large cardboard box with number puzzles, brain teasers, word problems to solve, vocabulary words to find meanings for, questions to find answers for, unfinished number stories, etc.

Place it on a table easily accessible to students. Add reference and resource materials, and you have a "think tank" ready to challenge those restless and intellectually curious students who always finish first and ask, "What's next?"

MATCH THE COMBINATIONS

Reviewing And Reinforcing Combinations

MATH

Prepare two identical charts by drawing lines on large sheets of heavy drawing paper or tagboard to make 18" x 24" boxes. Cut one chart apart to make small cards on which combinations may be printed with answers to the combinations on the back of the cards.

On the other chart, print answers to the combinations. (If possible, laminate the chart and matching cards.) Place the chart and cards in an interest center for free-time use. Instruct the students to work individually or in pairs to choose a card to answer the combination, then to turn the card over to check for the correct answer.

When the answer is correct, the card is placed answer-side up on the corresponding box on the chart. If the answer is incorrect, the card is placed in the student's "study stack." If used as a game, the student with the fewest "study stack" cards is declared the winner!

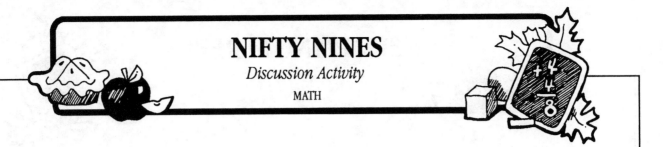

NIFTY NINES
Discussion Activity
MATH

Ask students to write the multiplication facts 1 times 9 through 10 times 9 on a sheet of paper. Ask them to look for an interesting pattern as they examine the multiplication table they have just written. Monitor how long it takes them to discover that the tens column in the products increases in order, but the ones column in the products decreases in order.

NIFTY NINES

$1 \times 9 = 9$
$2 \times 9 = 18$
$3 \times 9 = 27$
$4 \times 9 = 36$
$5 \times 9 = 45$
$6 \times 9 = 54$
$7 \times 9 = 63$
$8 \times 9 = 72$
$9 \times 9 = 81$
$10 \times 9 = 90$

For a bonus addition project, challenge students to add up the numbers in each of the three columns. Write answers for each addition challenge on a strip of paper and place it face-down in an easily accessible spot. As students finish adding the three columns, they may go to the answer strip and check their answers.

After all students have completed the activity, they might like to make up additional math challenges using the "Nifty Nines." Example:

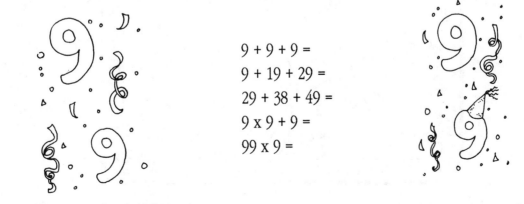

$9 + 9 + 9 =$
$9 + 19 + 29 =$
$29 + 38 + 49 =$
$9 \times 9 + 9 =$
$99 \times 9 =$

SHOPPING SPREE

Group Project

MATH

Provide newspapers with full page food ads and cookbooks with simple recipes. Ask students to work together in groups of three or four to plan a festive dinner for six or eight people. Instruct each group to write out a complete menu, and use the cookbooks to list the ingredients and the amount needed (of each) for the meal. Then have them write out shopping lists that include food to be purchased; to use the newspaper ads to find the costs of each item; and then find the total cost of the meal.

This is a good activity to use just before a holiday (planning a Christmas or Thanksgiving dinner) or it could be adapted for an individual homework project.

MATH • A • MAGICIAN

MATH AWARD

MEASURE UP
Teacher-directed Activity

MATH

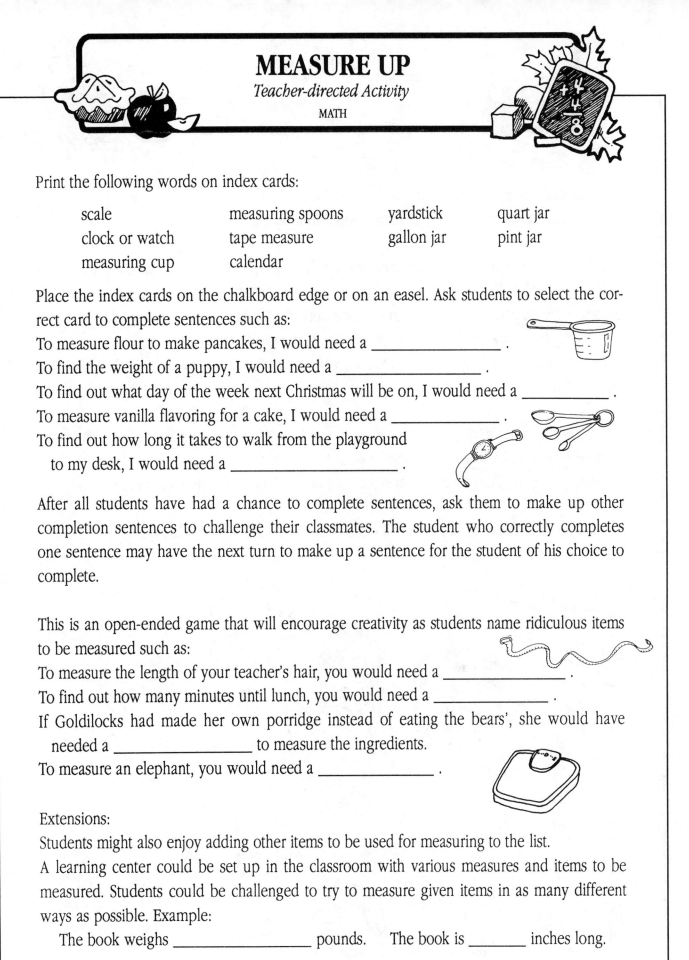

Print the following words on index cards:

scale	measuring spoons	yardstick	quart jar
clock or watch	tape measure	gallon jar	pint jar
measuring cup	calendar		

Place the index cards on the chalkboard edge or on an easel. Ask students to select the correct card to complete sentences such as:

To measure flour to make pancakes, I would need a _____ .

To find the weight of a puppy, I would need a _____ .

To find out what day of the week next Christmas will be on, I would need a _____ .

To measure vanilla flavoring for a cake, I would need a _____ .

To find out how long it takes to walk from the playground
   to my desk, I would need a _____ .

After all students have had a chance to complete sentences, ask them to make up other completion sentences to challenge their classmates. The student who correctly completes one sentence may have the next turn to make up a sentence for the student of his choice to complete.

This is an open-ended game that will encourage creativity as students name ridiculous items to be measured such as:

To measure the length of your teacher's hair, you would need a _____ .

To find out how many minutes until lunch, you would need a _____ .

If Goldilocks had made her own porridge instead of eating the bears', she would have
   needed a _____ to measure the ingredients.

To measure an elephant, you would need a _____ .

Extensions:

Students might also enjoy adding other items to be used for measuring to the list.

A learning center could be set up in the classroom with various measures and items to be measured. Students could be challenged to try to measure given items in as many different ways as possible. Example:

   The book weighs _____ pounds.   The book is _____ inches long.

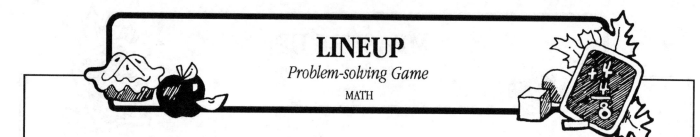

LINEUP
Problem-solving Game

MATH

Ask the students to form a line at the front of the room. Places in line may be determined by asking students to "number off" at their desks before lining up.

The last student in the "lineup" may be asked to be the "problem-giver" (or the teacher may assume this role). The first problem is given to the first student in the lineup. If he gives an incorrect answer, the next student in line attempts to give the correct answer. If this answer is correct, the two students change places. If neither student gives the correct answer, the game continues until one student gives the correct answer and moves to the "number one spot" in line.

The object is to get to the "number one spot" and stay there as long as possible. The game continues until each student has had several turns and "time" is called. The student in the number one spot at this time becomes the "problem-solver," and the game begins again.

This game provides a fun way to review math facts or to reinforce basic skills or concepts.

Let children help assign a number value to each letter of the alphabet. (Less mature children may need to simplify this activity by using numerals and letters in normal order A-1, B-2, C-3, etc., while more mature children would use scrambled order to provide interest A-5, B-2, C-10, etc.)

Print the letter/number code on a chart or the chalkboard to be used in finding the value of various names. The activity may begin with children finding the value of their own names and the names of classmates and progressing to finding the value of a list of names compiled by the teacher or the group. Example: the teacher, principal, school secretary, etc.; fictional characters from favorite stories; famous people, etc.

This activity could also be used as a party game with a printed list of appropriate words distributed with the numerical value of each letter and the first person to arrive at the value of each word determined the winner. Depending on the maturity of the group, the object of the game could be to find the total value of all the words on the list.

SIZE WISE
Group Game

MATH

This game can be played by a small group or by the entire class to help students strengthen their abilities to estimate measurements. It requires no materials, special setting or advance preparation.

One student is appointed as the first "size wise mystery person." He selects an object easily visible in the classroom and whispers the name of the object to the teacher. The "size wise mystery person" then gives two clues for the size of the mystery object.

Example: The size wise object is wider than my desk. It is not as wide as the teacher's desk. The size wise object is not as tall as the wastebasket. It is larger than the dictionary, etc.

Students then take turns trying to name the object. The student who successfully names the object becomes the next "size wise mystery person" and selects the next mystery project. Encourage students to use a wide variety of words by writing words such as the following on the chalkboard before the game begins:

long	small	narrow	big
short	large	wide	little
tall			

MATH REVIEW & REINFORCEMENT

Activity

MATH

Reproduce the math review and reinforcement tables on the following pages. Prepare and use the student activity table in the following manner.

1. Cut each sheet apart to make individual review tables.
2. Fold back the answer strip on the dotted line leaving room for students to write answers.
3. After answers have been written, the strip may be unfolded for self-checking.

The tables may also be reproduced and stapled together at the top to provide practice workbooks for homework or free-time use.

In this instance, a separate sheet of paper might be used for the answers so that the booklet could be used over and over as long as needed to meet individual student needs.

The same procedure could be used to make animated classroom booklets for use in student tutoring sessions, free-choice interest centers, or for individual practice.

MATH FACTS REVIEW
Multiplication

MATH

Multiplication (3)		Multiplication (4)	
$3 \times 1 =$	3	$4 \times 1 =$	4
$3 \times 2 =$	6	$4 \times 2 =$	8
$3 \times 3 =$	9	$4 \times 3 =$	12
$3 \times 4 =$	12	$4 \times 4 =$	16
$3 \times 5 =$	15	$4 \times 5 =$	20
$3 \times 6 =$	18	$4 \times 6 =$	24
$3 \times 7 =$	21	$4 \times 7 =$	28
$3 \times 8 =$	24	$4 \times 8 =$	32
$3 \times 9 =$	27	$4 \times 9 =$	36
$3 \times 10 =$	30	$4 \times 10 =$	40
$3 \times 11 =$	33	$4 \times 11 =$	44
$3 \times 12 =$	36	$4 \times 12 =$	48

MATH FACTS REVIEW
Multiplication

MATH

Multiplication (5)		Multiplication (6)	
5 x 1 =	5	6 x 1 =	6
5 x 2 =	10	6 x 2 =	12
5 x 3 =	15	6 x 3 =	18
5 x 4 =	20	6 x 4 =	24
5 x 5 =	25	6 x 5 =	30
5 x 6 =	30	6 x 6 =	36
5 x 7 =	35	6 x 7 =	42
5 x 8 =	40	6 x 8 =	48
5 x 9 =	45	6 x 9 =	54
5 x 10 =	50	6 x 10 =	60
5 x 11 =	55	6 x 11 =	66
5 x 12 =	60	6 x 12 =	72

MATH FACTS REVIEW
Multiplication

MATH

Multiplication (7)		Multiplication (8)	
7 x 1 =	7	8 x 1 =	8
7 x 2 =	14	8 x 2 =	16
7 x 3 =	21	8 x 3 =	24
7 x 4 =	28	8 x 4 =	32
7 x 5 =	35	8 x 5 =	40
7 x 6 =	42	8 x 6 =	48
7 x 7 =	49	8 x 7 =	56
7 x 8 =	56	8 x 8 =	64
7 x 9 =	63	8 x 9 =	72
7 x 10 =	70	8 x 10 =	80
7 x 11 =	77	8 x 11 =	88
7 x 12 =	84	8 x 12 =	96

MATH FACTS REVIEW
Multiplication

MATH

Multiplication (9)		Multiplication (10)	
9 x 1 =	9	10 x 1 =	10
9 x 2 =	18	10 x 2 =	20
9 x 3 =	27	10 x 3 =	30
9 x 4 =	36	10 x 4 =	40
9 x 5 =	45	10 x 5 =	50
9 x 6 =	54	10 x 6 =	60
9 x 7 =	63	10 x 7 =	70
9 x 8 =	72	10 x 8 =	80
9 x 9 =	81	10 x 9 =	90
9 x 10 =	90	10 x 10 =	100
9 x 11 =	99	10 x 11 =	110
9 x 12 =	108	10 x 12 =	120

MATH FACTS REVIEW
Addition

MATH

Addition (3)		Addition (4)	
3 + 1 =	4	4 + 1 =	5
3 + 2 =	5	4 + 2 =	6
3 + 3 =	6	4 + 3 =	7
3 + 4 =	7	4 + 4 =	8
3 + 5 =	8	4 + 5 =	9
3 + 6 =	9	4 + 6 =	10
3 + 7 =	10	4 + 7 =	11
3 + 8 =	11	4 + 8 =	12
3 + 9 =	12	4 + 9 =	13
3 + 10 =	13	4 + 10 =	14
3 + 11 =	14	4 + 11 =	15
3 + 12 =	15	4 + 12 =	16

MATH FACTS REVIEW
Addition

MATH

Addition (5)		Addition (6)	
5 + 1 =	6	6 + 1 =	7
5 + 2 =	7	6 + 2 =	8
5 + 3 =	8	6 + 3 =	9
5 + 4 =	9	6 + 4 =	10
5 + 5 =	10	6 + 5 =	11
5 + 6 =	11	6 + 6 =	12
5 + 7 =	12	6 + 7 =	13
5 + 8 =	13	6 + 8 =	14
5 + 9 =	14	6 + 9 =	15
5 + 10 =	15	6 + 10 =	16
5 + 11 =	16	6 + 11 =	17
5 + 12 =	17	6 + 12 =	18

MATH FACTS REVIEW
Addition
MATH

Addition (7)		Addition (8)	
7 + 1 =	8	8 + 1 =	9
7 + 2 =	9	8 + 2 =	10
7 + 3 =	10	8 + 3 =	11
7 + 4 =	11	8 + 4 =	12
7 + 5 =	12	8 + 5 =	13
7 + 6 =	13	8 + 6 =	14
7 + 7 =	14	8 + 7 =	15
7 + 8 =	15	8 + 8 =	16
7 + 9 =	16	8 + 9 =	17
7 + 10 =	17	8 + 10 =	18
7 + 11 =	18	8 + 11 =	19
7 + 12 =	19	8 + 12 =	20

MATH FACTS REVIEW
Addition

MATH

Addition (9)		Addition (10)	
9 + 1 =	10	10 + 1 =	11
9 + 2 =	11	10 + 2 =	12
9 + 3 =	12	10 + 3 =	13
9 + 4 =	13	10 + 4 =	14
9 + 5 =	14	10 + 5 =	15
9 + 6 =	15	10 + 6 =	16
9 + 7 =	16	10 + 7 =	17
9 + 8 =	17	10 + 8 =	18
9 + 9 =	18	10 + 9 =	19
9 + 10 =	19	10 + 10 =	20
9 + 11 =	20	10 + 11 =	21
9 + 12 =	21	10 + 12 =	22

MATH FACTS REVIEW
Subtraction
MATH

Subtraction (3)		Subtraction (4)	
$3 - 1 =$	2	$4 - 1 =$	3
$3 - 2 =$	1	$4 - 2 =$	2
$3 - 3 =$	0	$4 - 3 =$	1
$4 - 3 =$	1	$4 - 4 =$	0
$5 - 3 =$	2	$5 - 4 =$	1
$6 - 3 =$	3	$6 - 4 =$	2
$7 - 3 =$	4	$7 - 4 =$	3
$8 - 3 =$	5	$8 - 4 =$	4
$9 - 3 =$	6	$9 - 4 =$	5
$10 - 3 =$	7	$10 - 4 =$	6
$11 - 3 =$	8	$11 - 4 =$	7
$12 - 3 =$	9	$12 - 4 =$	8

MATH FACTS REVIEW
Subtraction

MATH

Subtraction (5)		Subtraction (6)	
5 - 1 =	4	6 - 1 =	5
5 - 2 =	3	6 - 2 =	4
5 - 3 =	2	6 - 3 =	3
5 - 4 =	1	6 - 4 =	2
5 - 5 =	0	6 - 5 =	1
6 - 5 =	1	6 - 6 =	0
7 - 5 =	2	7 - 6 =	1
8 - 5 =	3	8 - 6 =	2
9 - 5 =	4	9 - 6 =	3
10 - 5 =	5	10 - 6 =	4
11 - 5 =	6	11 - 6 =	5
12 - 5 =	7	12 - 6 =	6

MATH FACTS REVIEW
Subtraction

MATH

Subtraction (7)		Subtraction (8)	
7 - 1 =	6	8 - 1 =	7
7 - 2 =	5	8 - 2 =	6
7 - 3 =	4	8 - 3 =	5
7 - 4 =	3	8 - 4 =	4
7 - 5 =	2	8 - 5 =	3
7 - 6 =	1	8 - 6 =	2
7 - 7 =	0	8 - 7 =	1
8 - 7 =	1	8 - 8 =	0
9 - 7 =	2	9 - 8 =	1
10 - 7 =	3	10 - 8 =	2
11 - 7 =	4	11 - 8 =	3
12 - 7 =	5	12 - 8 =	4

MATH FACTS REVIEW
Subtraction
MATH

Subtraction (9)		Subtraction (10)	
$9 - 1 =$	8	$10 - 1 =$	9
$9 - 2 =$	7	$10 - 2 =$	8
$9 - 3 =$	6	$10 - 3 =$	7
$9 - 4 =$	5	$10 - 4 =$	6
$9 - 5 =$	4	$10 - 5 =$	5
$9 - 6 =$	3	$10 - 6 =$	4
$9 - 7 =$	2	$10 - 7 =$	3
$9 - 8 =$	1	$10 - 8 =$	2
$9 - 9 =$	0	$10 - 9 =$	1
$10 - 9 =$	1	$10 - 10 =$	0
$11 - 9 =$	2	$11 - 10 =$	1
$12 - 9 =$	3	$12 - 10 =$	2

SOCIAL STUDIES

IN THE TRAVEL BUSINESS
Creative Construction Activity
SOCIAL STUDIES

Have students design travel brochures which give as much information as possible about your city and/or state. Instruct students to include facts about population size, beautiful scenery, recreational opportunities and interesting history or folklore that would make a traveler want to visit the vicinity!

NEW SURROUNDINGS
Listing Activity
SOCIAL STUDIES

Instruct each student to make a list of ten things that a refugee in your state would need to know. Ask students to think about things such as state, federal and property taxes; election of officials; educational opportunities; recreational facilities; etc.

NEWS RECASTERS
Listening/Writing Activity
SOCIAL STUDIES

Bring a radio to class and have the students listen to a news broadcast. Allow only half of the students to take notes as they listen. After the broadcast, ask each student to write a news report presenting the news items of the broadcast and as many details about each item as possible. Divide the class into small groups, each group consisting of half "note-takers" and half "non note-takers." Have the students share and discuss their news reports and evaluate the benefits of reinforcing critical listening with written notes.

ON THE AIR
Dramatization
SOCIAL STUDIES

Instruct students to plan and present original "on-the-spot" broadcasts for:

1. the coronation of the queen of England
2. an olympic event in Stockholm
3. the aftermath of a tornado in Venezuela
4. other events and locations to be determined by the units being studied

DIGGING FOR GOLD

Research/Map Activity

SOCIAL STUDIES

Lead the class in a study of gold mining throughout the world (or silver, zinc or coal). Locate the world's significant gold mines on a map and string yarn from one location to another. Ask the students to find out how the metal is mined and shipped and what the most important worldwide uses of the metal are.

ANIMALS IN DANGER

Research/Creative Construction

SOCIAL STUDIES

Provide students with resource books to use in learning about the world's endangered species. Ask each student to make a list of endangered species and to develop a protection plan for one of the animals on the list. Have each student make a poster and bumper sticker designed to increase public awareness of the endangered animal's need for protection.

PROTECT THE TIGERS!

CARE FOR ♥ THE ANIMALS!

FOOD ON ICE
Research Activity
SOCIAL STUDIES

Direct students to study the history and development of fast-freezing foods. Ask the students to discover how this method of food preservation has influenced the world's food supply.

FACT FINDERS BOX
Research Skills Activity
SOCIAL STUDIES

Instruct the students to write interesting facts on 5'' x 7'' index cards. For example: The longest river in the world is the Amazon which has a length of 4,000 miles. Each student should write three things about or related to the fact on the same index card. Have the students sign and date their cards. Put the cards in a file box and place the box on a reading table. Encourage students to browse through the box and to add other facts periodically.

Note: This activity may be adapted to a bulletin board or TV program format.

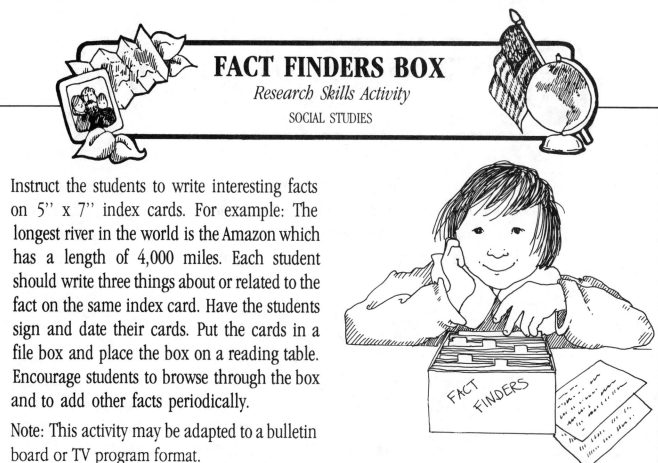

CITIES IN MOTION
Research/Mobile Construction
SOCIAL STUDIES

Print the names of major cities of the world on strips of paper. Fold the paper strips, place them in a basket, and have each student draw a city from the basket. Ask each student to research the city in order to use the city as the subject of a mobile. (This makes a great homework assignment.) Students may suspend construction paper drawings which show the city's uniquenesses and features from coat hangers, tree branches, wooden dowels, paper plates or aluminum pie pans. Hang the completed mobiles from the classroom ceiling for conversation pieces.

STUDENT'S POINT OF VIEW
Writing Activity
SOCIAL STUDIES

Ask each student to select a country to research. After gathering information, the student should write a report about life in that country as seen through the eyes of a student in that country. Included in the report should be a comparison and contrast to life in the student's own country. The report should also be illustrated with sketches or drawings of dress, food, lodging and other significant cultural facts.

After all reports have been presented, display the reports and illustrations on a bulletin board or table for further discussion.

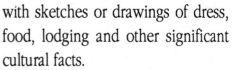

A SPECIAL EXHIBIT

Group Project
SOCIAL STUDIES

Direct the students to prepare a museum exhibit of artifacts related to the early settlement of the community. Ask faculty, staff and students in other classes to make contributions to the collection (for loan, of course). Have the students document each item by writing relevant dates, the item's history and the item's use or significance. Invite other classes to visit the exhibit. Appoint student guides to take turns leading visitors through the exhibit.

HOMETOWN ROOTS

Writing Activity
SOCIAL STUDIES

Ask each student to write and illustrate a legend about the settlement of your city. Ask students to include dates and events. Compile the stories into a book for the classroom library.

BLINDFOLDED EXPLORATIONS
Partner Experience
SOCIAL STUDIES

To develop students' awareness of the importance of eyesight for daily activities and to increase students' sensitivity to people with physical handicaps, involve the students in "blindfolded explorations." Ask students to work in pairs. Have one student of each pair wear a blindfold. The other student serves as a guide and helps the blindfolded partner find his way around the classroom. As the blindfolded student walks around furniture and classmates, he must try to identify classroom items by touch only. Then have the students switch roles. As a follow-up to the experience, ask the students to write about

how it felt to be "blind" and to have to depend upon and trust the sighted partner.

MEMORIES
Group Art Project
SOCIAL STUDIES

Let the class work together to make a large mural or chart highlighting the year's events (special programs, events, field trips, study units, etc.). Students may draw or paint pictures, write messages and brief stories, paste on magazine pictures and captions, etc. When the mural is completed, roll the paper into a scroll, tie it with yarn, and put it in a special place to be left for next year's class to enjoy.

WHO'S WHO
Interview/Writing Activity
SOCIAL STUDIES

Assign each student several school employees to interview so that all school employees are covered (teachers, custodians, secretaries, principal, cafeteria workers, etc.). Have the students write biographies for the persons interviewed. Prepare an interview sheet for the students in order to ensure completeness of information. Ask each writer to include colorful and original information to make the biographies as interesting as possible. Compile the biographies to make a "Who's Who In Our School" book. Let the students help design a cover, and then contribute the completed book to the school library.

OUR SCHOOL AS WE SEE IT
Creative Construction/Writing Activity
SOCIAL STUDIES

Let students work in small groups to make "guide booklets" designed to acquaint new students with the school. Ask students to include important or unusual features of the school building and the instructional program as well as unique activities of importance to the students. Allow the students to share and compare their guides. It will be fun to see how different students view the "important things" about the school.

FAMOUS PUPPETS
Construction/Play Presentations
SOCIAL STUDIES

Have students make paper sack or sock puppets to use in short plays about the lives of famous Americans (or famous world figures). Instruct the students to present enough information so that classmates are able to guess who the famous people are!

ROLE DESCRIPTIONS
Writing Activity
SOCIAL STUDIES

Write this activity on the chalkboard or pre-pare a pupil worksheet to be handed out to the students.

Name a country that has a:

President _____

King _____

Prime Minister _____

Write a role description for each position. Compare and contrast the three roles in a brief paragraph.

WHERE IN THE WORLD
SOCIAL STUDIES

Use resource books, maps and globes to find answers for these questions.

Where in the world . . .

1. is most of the world's diamond supply mined?
2. did the first banking system originate?
3. was democracy born and nourished?
4. did the last dinosaurs live?

5. did the first permanent American settlers come from?
6. was the first successful airplane flight launched?
7. is the longest man-made bridge located?

8. was the first space flight to the moon launched?
9. was the first printing press made?
10. is the Dead Sea located?
11. did the longest reigning monarch rule?

12. is the highest mountain peak located?
13. was the coldest temperature recorded?
14. are the seven wonders of the world located?
15. was the site of the last world olympics?
16. would you go if you could go anywhere in the world?

GETTING ACQUAINTED
Group Interaction Activity
SOCIAL STUDIES

This activity should be presented during the first week of school. Cut pennants out of bright colors of construction paper. Print one student's name on each pennant. On the first or second day of school, randomly distribute the pennants so that no one knows who has whose name. (Be sure that no student has his own name.) Inform the class that there will be a "getting acquainted" party on Friday. Instruct the students to observe the persons whose pennants they have and to secretly gather information about those persons. Have the students use their observations and information to decorate the pennants. During the "getting acquainted" party, allow each student to present his pennant and to give information about the person so that the other students may guess who it is. (Ask students to save all physical descriptions until the end.)

Example: "I present to you a girl who likes to cook, draw and read books. She goes camping with her family on weekends. She has a brother, two sisters and a cat. She laughs a lot, and she has many friends. This girl has red hair and green eyes.

When the class guesses who the person is, the pennant may be added to a bulletin board display.

FLAGS TO COLOR
SOCIAL STUDIES

Use resource books to find out what colors of crayons to use in order to correctly color each flag below.

Color the flags.

Be able to tell three important things about each country.

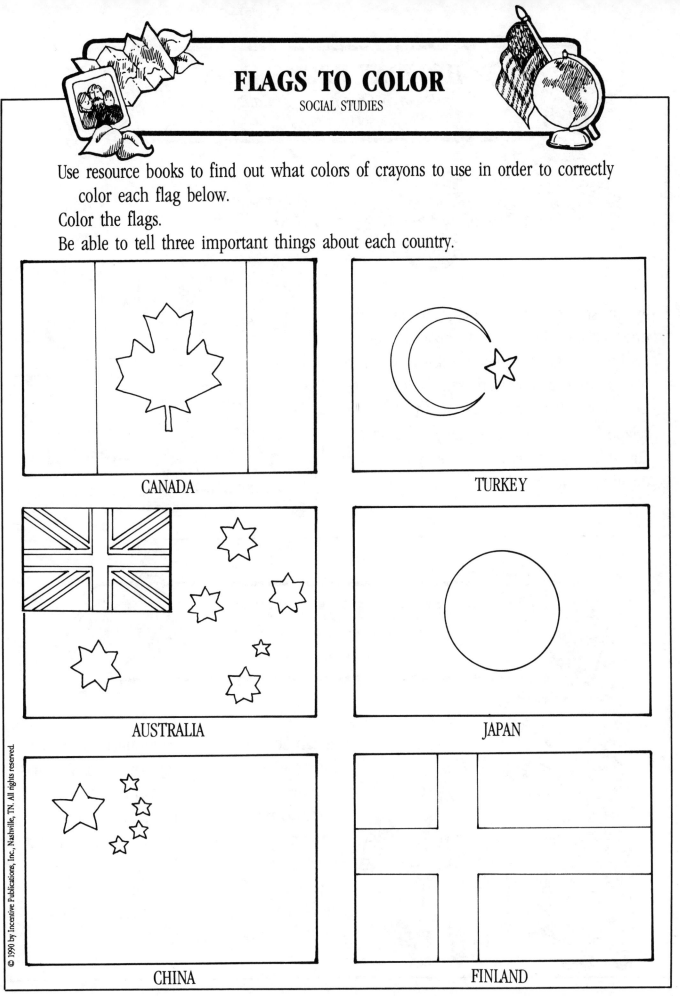

CANADA

TURKEY

AUSTRALIA

JAPAN

CHINA

FINLAND

HOLIDAY BEGINNINGS
Research/Creative Presentations
SOCIAL STUDIES

Assign student committees to research the origins and histories of major holidays celebrated in the community. Ask each group to plan an original way to present their findings to the class (such as a skit, an art project, a scrapbook, or even a class party). The important things to stress are creativity and thoroughness of information.

OUR COMMUNITY
Research/Writing Activity
SOCIAL STUDIES

Assign student research committees to gather information to use in preparing reports about various community organizations and institutions, i.e., number, locations, and denominations of churches; human service organizations; elementary and secondary schools; public parks; hospitals; etc. Compile all of the reports into an information booklet for the classroom reading table.

HIDDEN TRANSPORTATION
SOCIAL STUDIES

Circle and color six forms of transportation hiding in the picture.
Use the six forms of transportation to complete the sentences below.

1. To visit a country across the ocean, I would need to travel by _____ .

2. I could ride a _____ to visit a friend in my neighborhood.

3. If my class took a field trip, we would need to travel by _____ .

4. To "laze away" a sunny day on a lake, a _____ would be nice.

5. To visit national parks in two neighboring states, a family of four would probably travel by _____ .

6. Early American settlers traveled west by _____ _____ .

MEMORY ROUNDUP

SOCIAL STUDIES

- Write the full name of the mayor of your city, the governor of your state, and the president of your country.

- Draw and color the American flag. Be sure to include the correct number of stars and stripes.

- List ten classmates whose given names have two syllables.

- Draw a symbol for each of these five major holidays. Write the name of the month each holiday occurs beside the appropriate symbol.

- Draw and color a picture of your state flower, flag and bird.

- List three dates of importance to your country. Tell what occurred on each date.

- List the seven days of the week. Draw a weather symbol beside each day to show what the weather was like on that day last week.

COUNTRIES IN REVIEW

Research/Creative Construction

SOCIAL STUDIES

Ask each student to choose a country (other than his own) that he would like to visit. Instruct the students to gather facts and information about their chosen countries to use in preparing pictorial presentations of the highlights of the

countries. Direct students to fold large sheets of construction paper into six sections and to outline each section with a black crayon or marker. After numbering the boxes from one to six, each student may draw a picture of something of importance to the country in every box, i.e., flag, major industry, chief governing official, etc. Have the students label their pictures. Exhibit the completed projects on a bulletin board.

EXPORT/IMPORT

Listing Activity

SOCIAL STUDIES

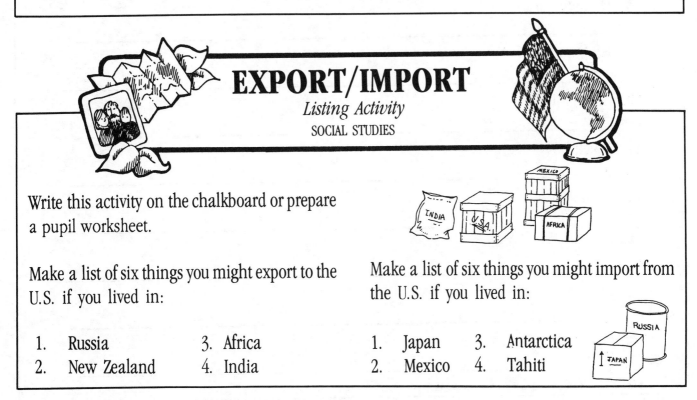

Write this activity on the chalkboard or prepare a pupil worksheet.

Make a list of six things you might export to the U.S. if you lived in:

1. Russia   3. Africa
2. New Zealand   4. India

Make a list of six things you might import from the U.S. if you lived in:

1. Japan   3. Antarctica
2. Mexico   4. Tahiti

DEFINITIONS ON THE LINE
SOCIAL STUDIES

Use resource books to help you find one-line definitions for the following terms. Write each definition on the line below the term.

1. Peninsula

_____

2. Municipality

_____

3. Democracy

_____

4. Intercoastal Waterway

_____

5. Cartography

_____

6. Prejudice

_____

7. Continental Divide

_____

8. Hieroglyphics

_____

9. Economics

_____

10. Bibliophile

_____

11. Legendary

_____

12. Immigration

_____

13. Partisan

_____

14. Critique

_____

15. Equator

_____

INVENTIONS OF IMPORTANCE
Research Activity/Skit Presentations
SOCIAL STUDIES

Have students work in groups to research the histories and uses of inventions that have greatly affected life today, i.e., electricity, airplane, telephone, morse code, cotton gin, computer, etc. Instruct the students to prepare skits for presenting their collected information to the class. Dates, names, places and events may be revealed in the skits, but the inventions themselves should not be identified. As each group presents its skit, the other students should try to guess what the invention is.

CARS AROUND THE WORLD
Map Activity
SOCIAL STUDIES

Present a unit on the development of the automobile industry. Use thumbtacks to locate on a classroom map the cities of the world which produce most of the automobiles today. Collect pictures of automobiles from early times until the present. Have each student write a creative story about one of the pictures.

RESEARCH, RESEARCH, RESEARCH
SOCIAL STUDIES

Use books and audio and video resources to find out about . . .

1. when, where, why and how the United States evolved from an agricultural society to an industrial society

2. the history and purpose of the United Nations, its participating countries, its current programs and its outlook for the future

3. the roles and goals of two or three well-known women involved in world politics

4. the influence of airplane bombers on the outcome of World War II

5. the establishment of early water routes across the mediterranean

6. the story of Columbus's voyage to America

7. the invention of the telegraph machine and its influence on world trade

8. the exploration of the world's natural resources for personal gain and organized efforts to limit or curtail future destruction

9. three career opportunities of interest to you and the talents, traits, requirements and rewards associated with each

10. the locations and histories of famous bridges of the world

11. the history of the polio vaccine and heart transplants, and the effects of each on world health

12. the obligations and responsibilities of the citizens of a democracy and the long and short-term consequences of a citizen's failure to uphold these responsibilities and obligations

13. the use of computers in everyday life and the possible changes brought about by computers within the next twenty years

NATIVE AMERICANS
Mural Activity
SOCIAL STUDIES

Present a study of the customs of native American Indians. Let students help create a large mural which illustrates the highlights of various tribes and commemorates their contributions to American life.

OUTSTANDING WOMEN
Poster Activity
SOCIAL STUDIES

Let the class help to make a list of at least ten famous American women. Have the students make posters depicting the lives and times of the famous women to be displayed on a bulletin board.

LOCATE THE SEAS
SOCIAL STUDIES

Write a number in the blank beside each letter to match the major seas of the world with their locations.

1. Adriatic

2. Aegean

3. Arafura

4. Baltic

5. Barents

6. Beaufort

7. Bering

8. Bismark

9. Black

10. Caribbean

11. Caspian

12. China

13. Coral

14. Dead

15. Hudson Bay

16. Mediterranean

17. North

18. Red

19. Sea of Japan

20. Sea of Okhotsk

— A. lake between Israel & Jordon

— B. area of northern Pacific between Alaska & Siberia

— C. part of Arctic Ocean, north of Alaska & Canada

— D. west of Japan

— E. arm of Mediterranean, southeast of Italy

— F. arm of Atlantic between northern Europe & Great Britain

— G. between Europe & Asia

— H. between Asia Minor & Greece

— I. between Europe & Asia, world's largest inland body of water

— J. inland sea between Arabia & Africa

— K. arm of Atlantic between North America & South America

— L. area of Pacific between Australia & New Hebrides

— M. in eastern USSR & Asia

— N. between New Guinea & Australia

— O. arm of Atlantic in northern Europe

— P. part of Pacific between Japan & the Malay Peninsula

— Q. inland sea in Northwest Territory, Canada

— R. area of Arctic, north of Norway & USSR

— S. in western Pacific

— T. inland sea bordered by Europe, Africa & Asia

Answer Key

SIGN SAVVY
SOCIAL STUDIES

Find and circle the "meanings" of the international signs in the word find puzzle. Write the correct word or words under each sign.

Words To Find:

airport	men	telephone
first aid	no smoking	women
handicapped	no trucks	
hill	school crossing	

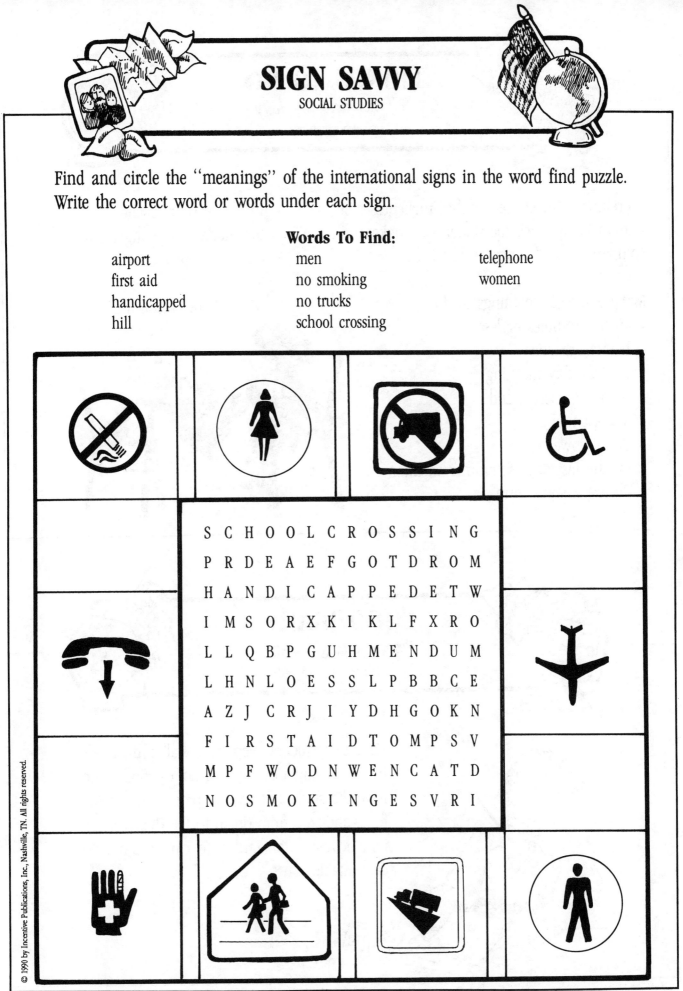

```
S C H O O L C R O S S I N G
P R D E A E F G O T D R O M
H A N D I C A P P E D E T W
I M S O R X K I K L F X R O
L L Q B P G U H M E N D U M
L H N L O E S S L P B B C E
A Z J C R J I Y D H G O K N
F I R S T A I D T O M P S V
M P F W O D N W E N C A T D
N O S M O K I N G E S V R I
```

Answer Key

THINGS TO DO
Self-awareness Activity
SOCIAL STUDIES

To reinforce the concept of the uniquenesses of human beings, ask the students to make and compare these "things to do" lists.

Make a list of ten things to do:
- in five minutes or less
- before breakfast
- on Saturday morning
- with your best friend
- after school
- on Halloween
- on the last day of summer vacation
- during a snowstorm
- to please your teacher
- to entertain a younger child
- on a class picnic
- to make a new friend
- when there is nothing to do

FOOD DIARY
Record-keeping Activity
SOCIAL STUDIES

Have each student keep a list of all of the foods he eats during a twenty-four hour period. Then have the students trace the progression of the foods they ate from origin to the dinner table, i.e., beans: from garden to can to stove to dinner table.

FIND FIFTY STATES
SOCIAL STUDIES

Find and circle the names of each of the fifty United States.

```
R H O D E I S L A N D T U C I T C E N N O C
E A O K L A H O M A A I N A V L Y S N N E P
N W Z M I C H I G A N E W H A M P S H I R E
I A S O U T H C A R O L I N A Z K S A N E T
A I H G E O R G I A Z X B T Q I M A O C S E
M I S S I S S I P P I A N P N A G R N A F N
Z W I S C O N S I N R E O D R E T R S M H N
G A O B L S J N D W A I I Y L H V N O O A E
Y K N H W M R K O Y L A L O D P A A N N K S
K S I S I A R A C L N A L A S K A O P T G S
C A L I F O R N I A N W K K U T R W E A A E
U R L R Y K A O X D P O J U E T A G R N T E
T B I W A D N G E Z T A H X H S U T H A O O
N E E N I Q H E M A S S A C H U S E T T S D
E N S R B A S R W M L S A I N I G R I V E A
K A O N T W T O E E V R N E V A D A C L N R
S L O U I S I A N A O G A M A B A L A M N O
F I D A H O B A N L T G N I M O Y W B Z I L
S M I S S O U R I O K L E Z U M A Q D Y M O
V E R M O N T N N W E S T V I R G I N I A C
S O U T H D A K O T A I X N E W J E R S E Y
```

Answer Key

HALL OF FAME
Research/Creative Construction
SOCIAL STUDIES

This activity may be tied directly to a unit of study such as sports, heroes or famous Americans, or it may be left "open" for students' own selections.

Discuss why persons might be nominated to a hall of fame. Then establish criteria for nominating famous persons for your classroom's very own hall of fame. Ask each student to select a well-known or famous person whose life he would like to research. After sufficient information has been gathered, each student should plan and create a poster which presents facts and events related to the life and times of the chosen nominee.

FREEDOM FOR ALL

SOCIAL STUDIES

Color the numbered spaces to find a symbol of freedom.

2 green   4 blue   5 orange   7 yellow

ENRICHMENT

ALPHABET ANTICS

ENRICHMENT

The following activities are "quickies" to be used to fill the ten or fifteen minute periods before lunch and at the end of the day, or to relieve boredom and restlessness in those "sure to occur" periods when time is too short for a real lesson but too long to waste.

Cut and paste each letter on an index card and file alphabetically in a file box.

Each idea may be presented as a chalkboard or verbal discussion activity for full-group participation; as an assigned pencil and paper project for individual students; as a small group project for students to compete against one another and the clock. Or, the file box may be placed in a learning center or free-time activity center for individual use.

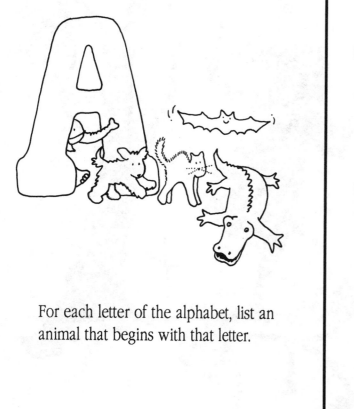

For each letter of the alphabet, list an animal that begins with that letter.

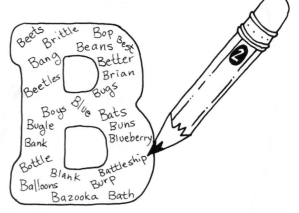

Draw the biggest capital "B" you can on a sheet of drawing paper. Fill the "B" with words that begin with "B."

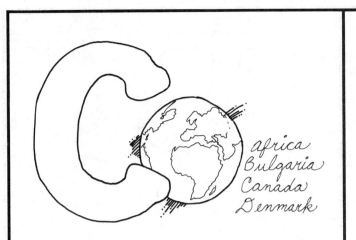

Write the names of twenty countries in alphabetical order.

Use your dictionary to design a word-find puzzle including 10 words that begin with the letter "D" and 10 words that end with the letter "D."

Extra! Extra! Read all about it. Read the editorial section of your newspaper. Write a letter to the editor agreeing or disagreeing with an idea expressed.

Find a friend to work with you to make a list of at least 15 words that name traits of a true friend.

List 10 great ideas for improving your study skills to help you get great grades.

Draw a hidden picture puzzle with pictures of 7 things whose names begin with letter "H" hiding in the scene.

Write 3 words beginning with each of the letters: a, e, i, o, u and y.

Write 2 words beginning with each of the letters: b, c, d, f, g, h, j, l, m, n, p, q, r, s, t, v, w and x.

Draw a big kite. Fill it with words beginning with the letter "K."

Write 12 words that contain more than one "L."

Write the names of 10 mother animals. Beside the name of each animal, write the baby animal's name.

List 9 numbers that begin with the letter "N."

In one times three minutes, list as many three letter words as you can that begin with the letter "O."

Draw pictures of 10 foods whose names begin with the letter "P."

Design a patchwork quilt with 26 squares. Draw a picture of something whose name begins with each letter of the alphabet in the squares.

Race with a friend to see who can write the most words with the letter "R" as the second or third letter in the word.

Write 10 compound words beginning with the word "snow."

Time yourself! In 10 minutes, write as many words as you can out of the letters in "Timex.®"

Draw pictures of 6 things you could stand under.

Write 7 words beginning with the letter "V" and ending with the letter "E."

List 10 words that could tell why something happened, list 12 words that could tell when something happened, and list 20 words that could tell where something happened.

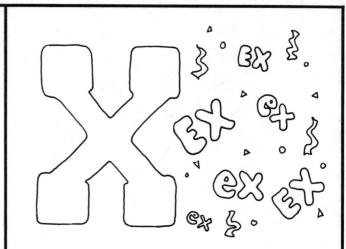

Write a dozen words beginning with the letter "E" and having the letter "X" as the second letter.

Draw and color a scene with pictures of 10 yellow things in the scene.

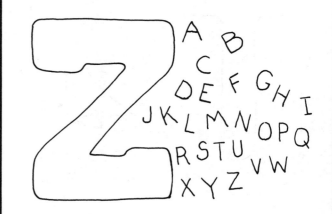

Make a word-find puzzle with 1 word beginning with each letter of the alphabet. Trade puzzles with a friend and see who can find the 26 words first.

RHYTHM ROUNDUP
Music Appreciation/Listening
ENRICHMENT

Snap, tap, clap, click and stamp to help students develop listening skills and music appreciation.

Clap the rhythm of familiar songs such as "Twinkle, Twinkle Little Star," "Three Little Kittens Have Lost Their Mittens," and "Mary Had A Little Lamb." Ask students to guess the name of the song and then join in repeating the clapping pattern. After several experiences, have students take turns clapping songs of their choice for others to guess.

Play recordings of familiar songs, and ask students to tap or stamp their feet, use pencils to tap out the rhythm on their desks, or repeat the patterns by clicking their tongues or snapping their fingers.

Interpretative movements for favorite songs such as "I'm a Little Teapot" and "The People on the Bus" allow children to relate physically to the rhythmic patterns.

Flexing, bending, swaying, stretching and nodding are all good "rainy day" activities to provide relaxation while reinforcing music appreciation.

Other creative movement activities that provide for rhythmic interpretation include: skating, trotting, arching, skipping and galloping. Students will enjoy bringing their favorite records from home to add to the classroom collection.

Have students tear construction paper (of one color only) and paste on white drawing paper to "illustrate" a feeling or emotion. For example, very thin pieces of black paper could be arranged to express fear. Other subjects could include happiness, loneliness, anger, frustration, grief, hope, greed, generosity, curiosity and pride.

When the art project is completed, ask the students to write a story about a situation involving the emotion or feeling expressed. Allow freedom for the story to center on fictitious characters or to recount a personal experience.

Prepare a bulletin board display to exhibit the collages and the stories. Arrange time for students to discuss both their own and their classmates' work, to discuss the feelings expressed, and to recall times and situations when they felt some of the same emotions.

PERSONALLY SPEAKING

- Nominate a classmate for the "Good Citizenship Award" by writing a paragraph which explains why you think that person should win the award. (Give specific facts.)

- List six things you would like to change about your school. Write why and how you would make each change and what you think the results of the changes would be.

- Make a "me poster" for the bulletin board. Write your name in the center of a sheet of drawing paper (make the letters as fancy as you like). Then, draw pictures around your name to show the important things about yourself (hobbies, ambitions, favorite school subject, favorite food and sport, etc.).

- "If I had a magic carpet to take me anywhere in the world, I would go . . ." Pretend that you have a magic carpet for three days. Tell where you would go and what you would do.

- Make a list of your self-improvement goals for the coming year. Put an "O" beside the goals you are working to achieve now and an "X" beside the goals you have not started working on yet.

- Design an original logo for your school which shows what you consider to be important about the school. Try to make the logo interesting to parents and teachers as well as to students.

- "If I were principal for a day, I would . . ." Write what you would do and why you would do those things if you were principal of your school for one day.

AN ADMIRABLE ALPHABET

ENRICHMENT

Write the name of a person whose actions or personality fit each word below. Write one sentence telling why this person qualifies for the admirable alphabet. You may use people from fiction, history or from real life today.

Active
Brave
Courageous
Daring
Energetic
Fearless
Giving
Honorable
Insightful
Just
Kind
Loving
Moral
Noble
Orderly
Positive
Quiet
Responsible
Strong
Truthful
Unselfish
Valor
Watchful
XY Zestful

A active. William

G giving

Q quiet Susie Lee is the most quiet person I have....

H honorable George Washington. President Washington was very well known for his honesty...

U unselfish

T truthful Leslie Meyers Leslie always tells the truth....

I insightful Madeleine L'Engle is a very insightful author....

R responsible

C courageous Crazy Horse. He was a Souix Indian....

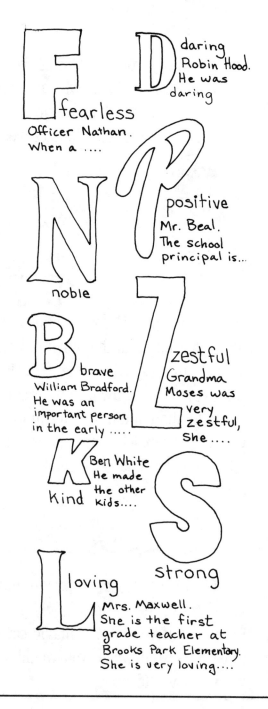

F fearless Officer Nathan. When a ....

D daring Robin Hood. He was daring

N noble

P positive Mr. Beal. The school principal is...

B brave William Bradford. He was an important person in the early .....

Z zestful Grandma Moses was very zestful, She ....

K Ben White He made the other kids.... kind

S strong

L loving Mrs. Maxwell. She is the first grade teacher at Brooks Park Elementary. She is very loving....

GALLERY OPENING
Art Exhibit
ENRICHMENT

Turn your classroom into an art gallery. Here's how!

• Plan the exhibit well in advance. Notify students of the theme and the entry guidelines as soon as possible. You will need to determine the art media to be used, any size restrictions for finished products, and the criteria to be used in judging entries (originality, attention to detail, neatness, etc.). Be sure that all students understand and are comfortable with the requirements!

• Appoint a panel of judges making sure none are related to any of the students, i.e., principal, school librarian, school secretary, local artist, etc.

• Invite an art teacher, a museum director or an art dealer to visit the class to discuss exhibit preparation, setup and judging procedures.

• Appoint or elect committees to mount and hang the entries, to publicize the exhibit, to provide "hospitality" during the exhibit (refreshments are a fun option), and to create a catalog containing information about each entry.

• Award ribbons for first, second and third place winners as well as recognition awards for all participants (see page 128).

• Appropriate topics for the exhibit might include:

The wonders of nature
Home sweet home
Scenes around town
On the go
Faces and places
Still life
Airborne

COLOR CAPERS

ENRICHMENT

- List 13 green vegetables. Make an "O" beside the ones you like and an "X" beside the ones you don't like.

- Think yellow! List five yellow foods, five yellow flowers and five yellow things you might see on the street.

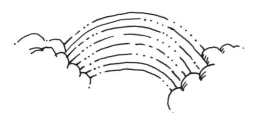

- Draw and color a rainbow. List the seven colors of the rainbow.

- List six people in your class who have blue eyes and six people who have brown eyes.

- List ten people in your class who have brown hair.

- Find three people in your room who are wearing one of the primary colors: red, yellow, blue. Make up a "colorful" story about those three people.

- Is your class a "Yankee Doodle Dandy" class? List the names of all of the people wearing something red, all of the people wearing something blue, and all of the people wearing something white.

- Write a "color description" of your teacher. Use as much detail and as many different color words as you can.

Just for fun, cook breakfast in your classroom to celebrate a holiday or a special class achievement. Bring a slow cooker to make oatmeal, an electric waffle iron or griddle for pancakes or waffles, or an electric skillet for scrambled eggs. If you have a convention oven, cinnamon toast would provide a science experience extraordinaire as students concoct, smell, taste and describe the sensory treat.

Add fruit or juice and whatever else your budget or parents' contributions allow, and you have a most positive start for the day.

A TERRIFIC TEACHING TIP
2. Maybe your students would prefer lunch.
ENRICHMENT

For lunch, each child could bring a vegetable or two, the teacher canned tomatoes, bullion cubes, the slow cooker and crackers, and the feast is on.

The most marvelous part of all about this activity is the tempting smell that will fill the classroom all morning! You will want to plan a late lunch so that the aroma of the excitement can be extended to the fullest. (Bowls, spoons and milk and cookies can be "requested" from the cafeteria staff or parents.)

Ask each student to select an item which is made in a foreign country. Tell the students that the item must be clearly identified as to the country of origin (label, tag, etc.). Have each student write a report about the item which includes some or all of the following things:

- raw materials used to make the item

- manufacturing or craft process used to make the item

- place where the item was made

- information about the people and products of the country

- reason the country ships the item to the U.S.

- reason the U.S. imports the item rather than produces it

- ways in which the item affects your life-style

Let one day be "world bazaar" day. Let each student present his item and report to the class. The report should include locations, facts about the production of the item, and notes on the economy, climate, and life-styles of the people. After all the reports have been given, display the items and reports on a table for everyone to enjoy.

Extension: Make a classroom collection of catalogs with items of international origin. Place the catalogs in a learning center or free-time activity center, and allow time for students to browse through the catalogs to locate items from many different countries. Ask them to compare prices, shipping charges and expected time of delivery from one country to another. Making and sharing "wish lists" could also provide an added learning bonus activity.

TERRIFIC TEACHING TIP
4. Play "We're off to the moon!"
ENRICHMENT

Say, "Let's pretend our class has been chosen to be the first ___ grade class to go to the moon. A special moon shuttle is being designed to take us there. Space in the shuttle will be limited, so each of us may take only one thing, and to conserve space, these items must be in alphabetical order."

I will begin with an "A." Each person in turn must then name something whose name begins with the next letter of the alphabet. As the game progresses, each person calls the names of all the items already named and adds their own.

Ready? I am going to the moon. I will take an apple with me. The next person in line must then name an item beginning with a "B." I am going to the moon. I will take an apple and a blanket with me.

The next person continues in the same manner adding a "C" word. The game continues until all students have had a turn.

As an additional feature of the game, the words named may be printed on a chart or on the chalkboard as they are called. After each player has had a turn, each person may tell why the particular item was selected.

This version of an old favorite will generate lively interaction as well as aid in memory retention.

TERRIFIC TEACHING TIP
5. Popcorn Popper
ENRICHMENT

Bring a popcorn popper to school and have a party.
Smuggle a little science into the fun by discussing what makes the corn pop and how the kernels change in size, shape and texture during the popping process.

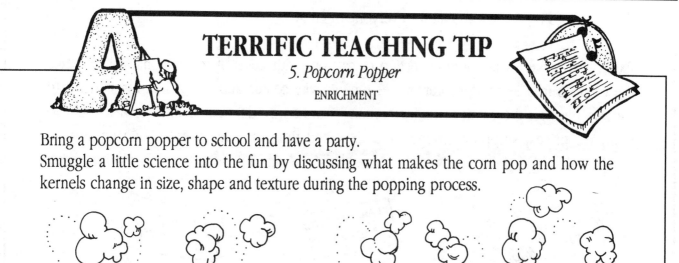

TERRIFIC TEACHING TIP
6. Make friendship jigsaw puzzles.
ENRICHMENT

Collect a stack of old magazines. Have students work in pairs to find pictures in the magazines to cut out, paste on construction paper, and cut into jigsaw puzzles.

Place the cutout puzzles in envelopes and write titles for the puzzles on the outside of the envelopes. The puzzles may then be presented to a classroom of younger children as a gift for their free-time activity center.

Travel magazines are good for this and numerous other creative activities. Ask parents and friends to contribute to your collection.

TERRIFIC TEACHING TIP
7. Plan ahead for an old-fashioned spelling bee.
ENRICHMENT

Allow students to contribute words to be spelled for several days in advance. Begin the list by writing words from the weekly spelling lists and from content areas on the chalkboard. Students may then add words of their choice to the lists. Lists may be copied and studied during this time.

On the day of the spelling bee, the list is erased, and the contest begins. As a student misspells a word, he is out of the match and must sit down.

The last person left in the match is declared the champion speller and may set the time and contribute the beginning word list for the next spelling bee.

TERRIFIC TEACHING TIP
8. Make rainbow-colored cakes.
ENRICHMENT

Have students collect all the broken and "almost used up" crayons in the room. Peel off all the paper and break the crayons into very small pieces. Put the pieces in paper muffin cup liners. Use the tinfoil type if you can get them, and use two or three paper liners for extra strength in each muffin cup.

Place them in a muffin pan. Take the pan to the cafeteria, and ask a cafeteria helper to place it in a slow oven and leave it all afternoon.

At the end of the school day, collect the muffin pan and leave it to cool overnight. The next morning the students will be pleased to have a collection of rainbow-hued colored cakes to add to their classroom art supply collection.

Of course you will want to celebrate by declaring a special rainbow art project time.

TERRIFIC TEACHING TIP
9. Clothesline Exhibit
ENRICHMENT

String a clothesline under the chalkboard ledge. Attach enough clothespins for each student; then designate each student's space on the clothesline exhibit. Students can hang artwork, special items brought from home, or any other materials they wish to exhibit. Encourage them to change their exhibits whenever they have something new to show the class.

TERRIFIC TEACHING TIP
10. Make Globes
ENRICHMENT

Provide each student with the following materials: balloon, reference books (textbooks, encyclopedias, etc.), tempera paint, paintbrushes, scissors, paste, newspaper strips, string and a black felt-tip marker.

After discussing the globe with the class, instruct the students to blow up their balloons and tie them with a piece of string about 18 inches long. Help the students paste newspaper strips on their balloons. (Note: It takes three layers of newspaper strips to form a sturdy paper ball.) Then have the students paint their balloons with tempera paint. Let the balloons dry overnight.

The next day, assist each student in drawing or tracing the seven continents, cutting them out, and pasting them in the appropriate places on the globe. Students may then use felt-tip markers to label the continents and oceans.

Hang the globes from the ceiling to create an interesting classroom climate. Later, allow the students to take the globes home for reference and reinforcement.

TERRIFIC TEACHING TIP
11. Read Aloud
ENRICHMENT

Read *Alexander And The Terrible, Horrible, No Good, Very Bad Day**. As a follow-up, share a terrible, horrible, very bad, no good day of your own. Then allow time for students to tell about days they have had where everything went wrong and nothing seemed to come out right.

In addition to the fun of listening to other students' experiences, it will be reinforcing for members of the group to be reminded that their friends, too, (including the teacher) sometimes have less-than-perfect days.

* by Judith Viorst, Atheneum, 1972.

TERRIFIC TEACHING TIP
12. Fantastic Feely Box
ENRICHMENT

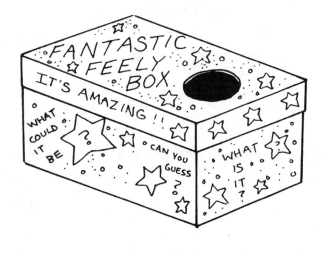

Make a sensory "feely box." Cut a hole (large enough for a student's hand) in the top of a shoe box. Place objects with various shapes and textures inside the box such as a scrap of velvet fabric, spaghetti noodles, a pocket mirror, a fastened safety pin, a coin, etc. Label the box "Fantastic Feely Box" and place it in a science center or on an exploration table. Have students reach into the box, feel the items inside, and try to identify each object.

TERRIFIC TEACHING TIP

13. Theme Days
ENRICHMENT

Theme days are always winners.

Here are suggestions to get you started. You and your students are sure to think up many more creative and exciting ones. Take time out to brainstorm and make a list of themes unique to the group. When things are getting a little dull, select a theme and plan a special day.

1. Good Nutrition Day - Have students bring a sample of their favorite nutritional snack to share with the class. Discuss the nutritional value of the snacks and why and how they contribute to good health.

2. Be Good To The Environment Day - Have students bring biodegradable and nonbiodegradeable materials to class. Discuss the differences in these materials and ways they can be improved. Discuss the effects of the materials on the environment. Ask students how they will care for their environment in the future.

TERRIFIC TEACHING TIP

14. *Each one teach one day.*
ENRICHMENT

Students are assigned partners to help them review, reinforce or learn basic skills and concepts. Pairs are formed the day before, and a planning time is provided so that special materials and plans may be organized.

The goal is for students to share strengths, weaknesses and resources for mutual benefit. A lasting byproduct of this day will be the friendships formed and the understandings built.

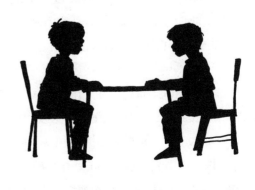

TERRIFIC TEACHING TIP
15. Color Day
ENRICHMENT

Think purple! Ask students to wear something purple, to bring purple articles to share, draw or paint purple pictures, write stories containing the color purple in the major plot or theme, make purple drink mix, serve grapes and/or eggplant for lunch, and have a contest to see who can list the most purple things in ten minutes. The list will go on and on as students dream up ways to "think purple."

TERRIFIC TEACHING TIP
16. Celebrate the big world we are a part of.
ENRICHMENT

About a week before the celebration, ask each student to select a country to represent. Provide a wide variety of resource materials including: textbooks, magazines, travel brochures, bulletins, maps, globes, atlases, encyclopedias, etc., keeping with the students' readiness and interest levels.

Ask the students to research the countries of their choice and to make a list of customs, climatic conditions, historical and current events, and other facts related to the countries from which their report can be made.

On the designated day, students may come in native dress; present artifacts and/or pictures representative of their countries; share a food, game, or special holiday or ceremonial custom; or tell about the country's economic or political condition and relay other interesting information gleamed from their research.

Have children bring boxes of all shapes and sizes to be used on box-a-traption day.

When the collection is sufficient and ranges from small jewelry boxes, candy boxes, and shoe boxes to coat boxes, grocery cartons, and even appliance boxes, set the date, and gather supplies for the big event.

In addition to the boxes, supplies should include: scissors, paste, crayons, markers, paints and brushes, tape, colored paper and "good junk" such as paper clips, buttons, yarn, sticks and stones and gadgets galore.

Ask students to work in groups of four or five to conceive and construct the box-a-traptions. Each group should begin by choosing a selection of boxes to use (or the boxes may be randomly distributed) and look at the boxes and brainstorm the "thing" to make. Then the fun begins.

As the boxes are stacked first one way then the other, pushed, pulled, fitted and refitted together, the idea for the final creation will emerge. The only rule is the boxes must be used "as is." They may not be cut or altered in shape or size.

The decorations, however, may be cut, colored, pasted or secured to the box-a-traption in any shape, size or manner desired.

When the original designs are completed, they should be named and placed on display for all to admire. Awards could be given by a panel of outside judges (school secretary, principal, etc.) for the "Most Imaginative," the "Most Realistic," and/or the "Most Outstanding" creation.

On this day, students should be asked to think of as many ways possible to raise school awareness and promote positive school spirit, not just in their own classroom but throughout the entire school. One group of students might decorate a bulletin board in the front hall to call attention to school rules. One in the cafeteria might encourage good manners and courteous lunchroom behavior. A third group might develop a poster for the gym or playground listing rules of good sportsmanship and fair play.

Arrangements could be made for a general assembly program where a pep rally could be staged and the school alma mater sung.

Language arts and social studies assignments might include: individual letters to parents focusing on school appreciation, writing a school history, newsletters to inform the community of school honors, events and schedules, or beginning scrapbooks with accounts of important events of the year (both past and present).

School pennants could be made and hung in the halls, and banners or balloons could be used to decorate classroom doors and windows. A brand new cheer, songs and class logos could be developed to add "spice" to the day.

This day is one everyone in the group will be sure to remember for a long time. Begin the day by reviewing the daily schedule so that the last activities of the day take place first thing in the morning and the schedule continues in this manner for the entire day. You may not be able to alter library, lunch, P.E. or events taking place outside the classroom, but you may be surprised how much flexibility there is in your daily schedule.

Allow children to wear some articles of clothing backward or inside out (only if they choose), to carry books "outside" rather than inside their book bags, and to greet each other with "good-bye" rather than "hello."

Number spelling or math papers with the number needed for the exercise, then begin with the last number and end with the first. Example: If you have sixteen words on a weekly spelling test, give out word number sixteen first and word number one last (number one should be the last word written on the paper).

Provide answers to math problems instead of the problems. Students are to "find" the problems rather than the answers.

Have dessert first for lunch. Tell a story from back to front. Example: Goldilocks ran all the way home promising herself that she would never again go into a house without an invitation. Before that …

TERRIFIC TEACHING TIP
20. Library Day
ENRICHMENT

On this day it's "three cheers for the library" all day long. If possible, make arrangements for a special visit to the public library nearest the school. Ask the librarian to talk with the students about the goals and services of the library. Also, arrange for all students who do not possess a library card of their own to make an application for one at this time.

If possible, provide for each child to leave the library with a book of his choice.

If a field trip to a public library is not possible, follow the same procedure using the school library. Back in the classroom, students might make bookmarks, design bookplates, and work in pairs to make posters for the school library.

No library day would be complete without a "book sharing time." Encourage creativity by suggesting that books be shared through dioramas, drama, posters, puppet plays, peep boxes or in "nonboring book report" fashion.

TERRIFIC TEACHING TIP
21. Have a "something beautiful" day.
ENRICHMENT

Ask each child to bring from home one thing he considers beautiful for a special sharing time. Emphasize that the "something beautiful" should be selected because of its special qualities, not because of its value. Example: A book of poetry because the words are beautiful when read aloud; one single daisy in a bottle; a string of glass beads because the colors are so vivid; a pinecone or seedpod; a piece of gift wrap or fabric because of the color and type pattern; a sack of hard candies because of their colors and taste.

Once the items are shared, each student should tell why the particular item was selected. After sharing, the items may be placed on a special table to be admired and discussed for the rest of the day.

TERRIFIC TEACHING TIP

22. "Show And Tell" Activity

ENRICHMENT

Let one day of the week be "Science Surprise Day." Friday is a good day for this because students will have ample time during the week to discuss the upcoming surprises and will be able to enjoy and inspect the surprises from the previous week.

Ask students to look for science-related objects to bring to class as "surprises" for the science table. Instruct the students to bring their surprises in brown paper bags (with no visible clues). At a designated "science surprise" period, each student presents his bag by saying, "Guess what I have in my bag," and gives three good clues as to the bag's contents. Acceptable clues include such things as living or nonliving objects; plant, animal, or mineral; stated use or function; place of origin; physical descriptions; etc. The student who guesses what is in the bag may place the object on the science table and take the next turn.

Plan a health fair! (For your class only.) Choose a day for the health fair and notify the students well in advance. Ask each student to prepare a project entry related to health such as a report, display, art project, experiment, etc. Exhibit the health projects on the day of the fair, have the students vote for the best entries, and award prizes to the winners. Invite a resource person, i.e., doctor, nurse, dental hygienist, technician, etc., to visit the class to discuss good health habits, careers in the health field, and/or health-related issues. Take the students outside for fun relays, games and

physical exercise. Healthy refreshments such as apple wedges spread with peanut butter and fruit juice are a nice finishing touch!

SUGGESTED HEALTH FAIR TOPICS

aerobic exercise

cells - bacteria

cells - contagious diseases

dental health

digestive system

drugs and their effects on the
    human body

endocrine system

first aid

five senses

health careers

health research

human body

human heart

muscular system

nervous system

nutrition

nutritional value of
    junk food

organically grown foods

pollution

public health

respiratory system

skin care

tobacco: effects on the
    human body

vitamins and minerals

World Health Organization

HEALTH FAIR AWARD

To: _____

For: _____

_____

_____

signed _____

date _____

TEACHERS' TOOLBOX

STAR SPANGLED STUDENT AWARD

To: _____

For: _____

_____

_____

_____   _____
date   signed

SUNSHINE AWARD

To: _____

For A Cheerful Disposition And Sunny Smiles as observed on _____

by _____

ALL MY WORK IS DONE!

100% CLUB

STAR READER · STAR READER
STAR READER · STAR READER

SELF-CONCEPT AWARD

TOOLBOX

Proud as a Peacock Because

has

_____

_____

_____

signed

date

SELF-AWARENESS AWARDS

TOOLBOX

I'M
IMPROVING IN

— — — — — — —

MY TEACHER IS
PROUD OF ME!

I'M A WINNER

I DID IT!

HAPPY HOMEWORK
SUGGESTIONS
TOOLBOX

1. Write a history of your town.

2. Make a list of rhyming words. Use them to write some fun poems.

3. Interview the oldest person in your family about his childhood.

4. Count the clocks and watches or the windows and doors in your home. Have a contest to see who in your family guesses closest to the number of clocks and watches or windows and doors.

5. Design awards for special traits or deeds in your family. Example: "World's Greatest Cook," "Cheerful Smile," "Neat Kid," etc.

6. Write a story about a "pretend trip." Use a long-ago setting, a space setting or a "make-believe never could be" setting for your story.

7. Review all your math facts. Make flash cards or review sheets if you need to "brush up."

8. Look in the refrigerator or pantry for some vegetables to use for a creative project. Try to think of some new things to do with them. Maybe you could make animals or characters, vegetable prints, "plant" one or two in a pot, or even make a pot of vegetable soup.

9. Look around your house for bottles, cans, newspapers, etc., that could be recycled. Gather these things together and deliver them to a designated recycling spot.

10. Do a secret good deed for every member of your family. See how long it takes each person to find out "who did it."

11. Pretend you have won one million dollars on a TV game show. Make a list of what you would do with the money in the order that you would do it. Ask a friend or family member to do the same thing and compare your lists.

12. Draw or paint a self-portrait. Hang it on your wall.

13. Read a biography of a famous person.

14. Keep a diary for one week. You'll be surprised at how interesting your life is.

ANIMAL NAMES FROM A TO Z

Resource List

TOOLBOX

A
aardvark
albatross
antelope
ape
armadillo

B
baboon
bat
bear
beaver
bird
bison
bobcat
buffalo

C
camel
cat
cheetah
chicken
chimpanzee
chipmunk
cougar

D
deer
dingo
dog
dolphin
donkey
dove
duck

E
eagle
elephant
emu

F
falcon
ferret
finch
fish
fox
frog

G
giraffe
gnu
goat
goose
gopher
gorilla
groundhog
grouse

H
hamster
hare
hawk
hen
hippopotamus
hog
horse
hyena

I
ibex

impala

J
jackal
jackrabbit
jaguar

K
kangaroo
koala

L
lamb
lemming
leopard
lion
llama
loon
lynx

M
marmot
mink
mole
mongoose
monkey
moose
mouse
muskrat

N
numbat
nyala

O
opossum

orangutan
oryx
ostrich
otter
owl

P
panda
parakeet
parrot
peacock
pelican
penguin
pig
platypus
porcupine

Q
quail
quetzal

R
rabbit
racoon
rat
raven
rhea
rhinoceros

S
sable
seal
sheep
shrew
skunk

sloth
squirrel
stork
swan

T
tasmanian devil
thrush
tiger
turkey
turtle

U
uakari

V
vole
vulture

W
wallaby
walrus
weasel
whale
wolf
wolverine
wombat
woodchuck

X

Y
yak

Z
zebra
zorille

INDEPENDENT PROJECT PLAN

TOOLBOX

Topic: _____

Type of project (circle one):   experiment   research   other

Hypothesis: _____

_____

_____

Date to begin: _____ Date to finish: _____

Materials: _____

_____

Procedure: _____

_____

Results: _____

_____

Conclusion: _____

_____

_____

_____
Name

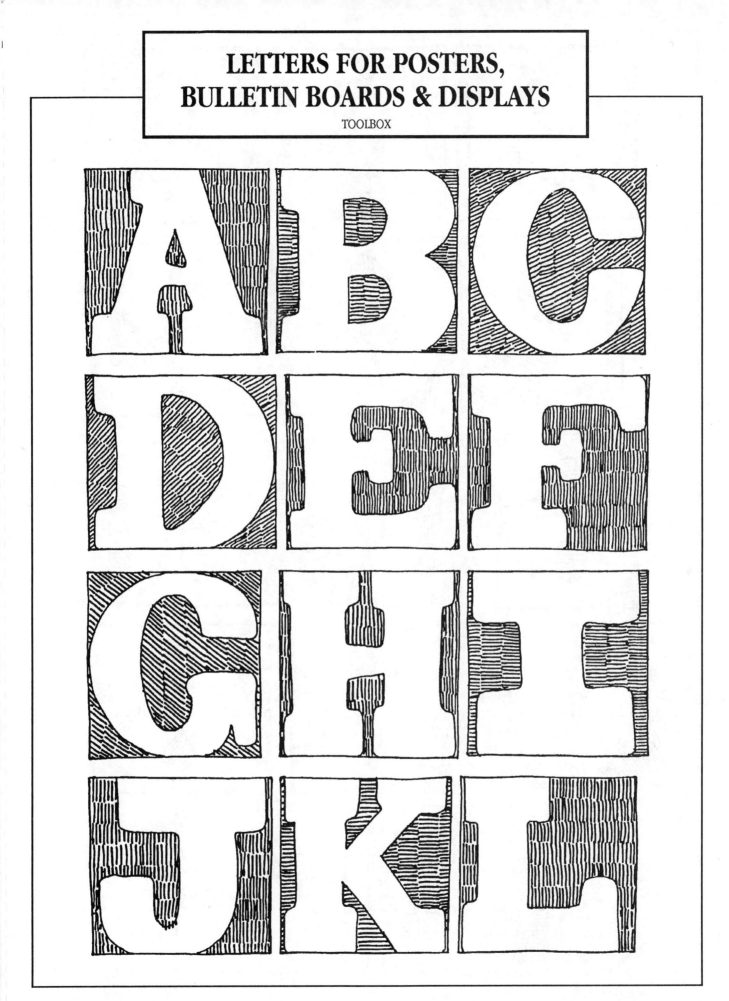

ANSWER KEY

Page 15

```
E X T R A O R D I N A R Y   E
X A Z E X C U R S I O N D   D X
T G E X E R C I S E H I J   T
E X P O S E E X T R E M E   R
M M U T B F M R C E X T R A   A
P T Y I E P D I L D O M E   C
O R E X C I T E E X A L T X   T
R E X T E N T X E S N K H   A
A L M L E Z E A X V D W A   K
N E A O X E X C E L R C U   R
E X P L I C I T R H I A S   R
O I J O S Y L G T V M D T   B
U T Z P T W E X C U S E O   F
S B E X T I N C T J Y N U   S
```

The performance was very well-done, even though it was
extemporaneous .

The theater had only one exit .

Page 25

Unscramble the Christmas words.

1. T I G F
   __gift__

2. Y E M R R
   __merry__

3. C R O D A F I T N O S
   __decorations__

4. T S A R
   __star__

5. A S T N A   S L A C U
   __santa claus__

6. D E R I N E R E
   __reindeer__

7. L E C B R E A I T N O
   __celebration__

8. G L E A N
   __angel__

Spooktacular words to find:

bat   mask   cat   witch
spook   costume treat   jack-o'-lantern
ghost   trick   goblin

Color by symbol to find a Thanksgiving surprise.

orange ◆   brown ●
red ♥   green ✿

Find and circle 4 elves hiding in the picture.

Page 26

```
A K D F I O C U M U L U S S N
W I C D H P L E C S A P E N O I
K T H E R M O M E T E R V O M B
M N Q W A D U B I O L E B W U S
V C H A I L D L O R H S M I U
E R I X N R S I O M G S E D D
L F O G J T B Z L B H U Y A C
O R U A O H K Z J O U R X X N I
C O I I F U B A R O M E T E R I
I S C L M N Z R U L I C E M R U
T T I S G D P D G A D W C O M S
Y R C L M E D Z O Y I I D M R
M I L D R S L E E T N Z E C U
H S E G A O S U N N Y D E T F
T A W B C T D V I J L A S E R
L I G H T N I N G B O U P R E
```

Anemometer	Grim	Snow
Barometer	Hail	Sleet
Blizzard	Humidity	Sunny
Cirrus	Ice	Rain
Clouds	Icicle	Storm
Cumulus	Laser	Thunder
Dew	Lightning	Thermometer
Fog	Mild	Velocity
Frost	Nimbus	Wind
	Pressure	

Page 51

```
D U C K L I N G   G
I   C A   I X E N W   O
K   H A L   T Q W W   S
S   I L F   T B M A   L
R   C L A   E U R F   I
M   K A N   C S M   N
P I G L E T   E   G
```

goose	__gosling__
lioness	__cub__
doe	__fawn__
sow	__piglet__
hen	__chick__
nanny	__kid__
duck	__duckling__
ewe	__lamb__
heifer	__calf__
cat	__kitten__

Page 57

1. owl
2. cardinal
3. jay
4. eggs
5. fly
6. worms
7. nests
8. south

Page 109

Page 108

A. 14	F. 17	K. 10	P. 12
B. 7	G. 9	L. 13	Q. 15
C. 6	H. 2	M. 20	R. 5
D. 19	I. 11	N. 3	S. 8
E. 1	J. 18	O. 4	T. 16

Page 111

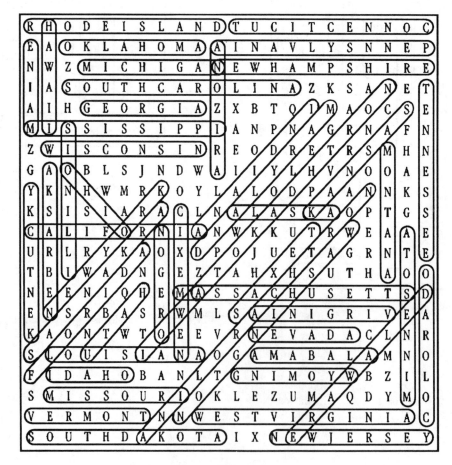

INDEX